FROM THE LIBRARY OF

All-American Boy

A Memoir

Scott Peck

Scribner
New York   London   Toronto   Sydney
Tokyo   Singapore

SCRIBNER
Rockefeller Center
1230 Avenue of the Americas
New York, NY 10020

The names and characteristics of some individuals
in this book have been changed.

SCRIBNER and colophon are
trademarks of Simon & Schuster Inc.
Designed by Meryl Levavi/Levavi & Levavi
Manufactured in the United States of America

10   9   8   7   6   5   4   3   2   1

Library of Congress Cataloging-in-Publication Data
Peck, Scott, date.
   All-American boy : a memoir / Scott Peck.
      p.   cm.
   1. Peck, Scott, date.   2. Gay men—United States—Biography.   3. Gay men—United States—Family relationships.   4.
Parents of gays—United States.   5. Fathers and sons—United
States.   6. Homosexuality—United States—Religious aspects—
Christianity.   7. Homophobia—United States—Religious as-
pects.   I. Title.
HQ76.8.P43A3   1995
305.38'9664'092—dc20
[B]   94-45480   CIP
ISBN 0-02-595362-1

Michelle

All-American
Boy

o n e

Somewhere in this night, it is all still happening.

We sit together on the grass, we three. My mother, her dancer's legs drawn up tightly against her chest, her face looking old in the glow of our block's lonely street lamp.

Quiet. She is quietly afraid, quietly listening for sounds from the porch where he sits—her husband, my stepfather. I can see the red tip of his cigarette, flaring on cue every two minutes as he inhales, flaring and sending illuminated little butterflies twitching to the floor. He sits in darkness, still and silent in his rocking chair, like some Mayan king, while his wife and children huddle closely together on the grass of the front lawn. Floridian night breezes, soaked in the smell of gardenias, lap around our heads and necks, chilling.

He will dictate this night to us; we wait for his decree.

When he stands, we scatter like frightened sparrows, Mother grabbing each of us by a wrist and moving out toward the sidewalk.

"Get ready," she hisses.

Without a word, he walks to the screen door, takes one final, spitefully deep drag, flicks the dying cigarette out in our direction and, turning, stumbles into the house. He is a giant's silhouette, the broad, bare back of my enemy—and the smoke from his lungs follows him, I think, like a serpent's tail.

For a while we sit, swatting at the tiny winged insects barefoot Southern boys call no-see-ums. The children on our block call them no-sees; and I feel like a no-see, safe and invisible in the shadows with my mother and my younger stepsister, Lisa.

Our whispered conversation is slow and meaningless, drawn out over the night, the danger, the obvious, stretching words that spread like a jasmine thicket to distance us from fear.

But when our mother speaks at last, the jasmine sours, the night is yanked away like a warm blanket on a freezing morning, and the blood and adrenaline pumping into our veins, pounding in our ears, quickly restrings the muscles in my ten-year-old stomach with an old familiar dread.

"I think he's asleep."

"Not yet," I said. "Give him more time."

"No, he's asleep. As drunk as he was, he's asleep by now."

"Can we go inside?" Lisa asked, and I hated her for it. Lisa, Rodney's "real" daughter, Lisa-who-was-real. She was his family, his "blood," whether he was sober or drunk, and she knew she was safe. Usually.

"Of course." And Mother's voice was mercy. Reassurance and mercy and just enough caution. "I'll just go in first, to make sure everything is alright."

"Don't," I said. "Don't. Don't go. He's awake."

"I'll be fine," she said as if speaking to convince a child instead of to convince herself. "I'll just poke my head inside the door."

She eases up the steps to the porch, walking over ashes and invisible eggshells to the front door. I hear its whine and help Lisa up in case we need to run. Mother's back disappears into the shadows inside the door frame, and I whisper a quick prayer, a child's prayer. O God, remember, O God, remember me . . .

"Rodney?"

O God, in your mercy, remember, remember me . . .

"Rodney?"

In the name of your Son, Jesus, I pray, sweet Father, remember . . .

An explosion. Jesus is coming soon.

She is screaming, and I think for one split-fractured second that a bomb has gone off in the living room. Breaking wood and shattering glass and my mother flying out onto the lawn like a shrieking ghost in her white nightgown.

He is close behind.

Lisa? Lisa. Someone's lit a match, Lisa, someone's lit a match. And the world is made of straw.

My sister and I sprint toward the family car and hide behind it, crouching low, eyes white and wide peering out over the hood to see what is happening.

She is face down on the lawn, and he is straddling her, stripped to the waist, his arm working, arcing through the air, his black leather belt cutting stripes on her back as she howls, as she begs him to stop.

She fights to her feet, arms stretched out behind her in desperate defense, vain defense, earning her new stripes. More screams, his blows relentless leather blurs, the sharp *crack!* of his belt and his drunken roars mixed in together, twisting and fighting and tearing out into this night and tearing into me.

She runs, and still he is on her. Nerves run between us, unseen wires cutting through the air, connecting our skin and our fear. My ass and legs throb in a familiar empathy every time his whip connects. It is me he is beating tonight; it may as well be me. She makes it to the concrete sidewalk, bolts down the street, and I think I can hear, as if from some safe distance, my own screams meeting hers as they fade past the street's yellow spotlight.

A universe unfolds and collapses in the time it takes him to stumble back to our house, talking and cursing to nothing and no one in weird counterrhythm to the clicking of the heels of his boots.

Don't move, Lisa. Don't. Move. Don't breathe. O Jesus, sweet Jesus, don't let him see . . .

He is inside. And we hear him lock the door.

Somewhere in this night I am still screaming.

She meets us halfway up the street, clutching the remnant of a shoulder strap he has ripped off. Lisa supports her on her left side, and I try to make her lean on me with her right.

"Mom, are you . . . ?" But she waves the words away as if they were no-sees.

"Just take me home," she says, and I wonder if I should tell her that the door is locked.

Our neighbor's house is safe, air conditioner eternally humming and rattling in a soothing way that only a Floridian can truly appreciate. We undress and get ready for bed, using toothbrushes set aside for us, familiar rituals. Sleeper sofas unfold, and Evelyn, our friend, rummages through closets for comforters and bedsheets. Evelyn is kind to us, even though she is a Catholic and will go to hell for that. We thank her politely, fascinated by the "devil's language" that pours so freely from her lips.

"Goddammit, Michelle, you've got to see a doctor."

"I'm fine."

"I can't believe what you take from that motherf—"

"Evelyn, please. The children. Be careful what you say. The children are always listening. I'm fine. Do you have any aloe?"

"Let me take you to the hospital."

"And explain this? They'd arrest him. Again. Besides, the children have school in the morning."

"Shit," Lisa mumbles, and I try very hard not to laugh.

We lay awake listening to the conversation that goes on until early morning, back and forth across our neighbor's kitchen table. No, I didn't think he was this drunk. No, divorce is not an option. No, I already tried. I already tried that. When she comes to bed at last, Lisa has already fallen asleep, because she is only nine, while I am ten. I fake sleep, pretending to stir only slightly when she begins to pray. She kneels on the floor, palms lifted timidly up to God in our church's tradition.

Somewhere in this night she is still praying.

And her voice is a living thing—a soft murmur rising then fading, as welcomed and as fragrant as the gardenias she planted by our porch. I can hear her gentle supplications, hear her Our Fathers, crystalline echoes of prayers she taught me long ago, prayers of forgiveness. Blessings to the enemy.

And I know that her faith is right. I know it fits the world like a missing fragment torn from some holy parchment; it fills the gaps between the lines, it makes the message clear.

". . . and forgive us our trespasses." The voice of a silent, suffering Nazarene. Take this cup from me.

". . . as we forgive those who trespass against us."

We forgive and are forgiven.

We forgive *to be* forgiven.

So I try and I try to forgive him.

But, O Christ in heaven—I have never hated with such perfection.

There were three men in my life. One was real and the other two were make-believe. I always preferred the fictions.

The first and most important was Jesus. Over our mantel, Mother hung a sign made of lacquered wood. In huge scrolled lettering, the type of calligraphy one finds in old King James Bibles, it read:

CHRIST IS THE HEAD OF THIS HOUSE

THE UNSEEN HOST OF EVERY MEAL

THE SILENT LISTENER AT EVERY CONVERSATION

Beneath the sign, Reality would sprawl out in his La-Z-Boy recliner and watch television. Mother talked to him, scurrying back and forth from the dining room to the kitchen, her hip bumping open the swinging door connecting the two rooms, her hands shrouded in Holly Hobbie cooking mittens, carefully balancing casseroles or trays of pork chops and the requisite country biscuits.

She talked to him about her day, about church, about her trip to the supermarket, back and forth, as if anyone were listening, while Rodney picked his teeth and watched *Three's Company*, his face sunburned from a day of hanging drywall on the construction site, his expression something short of disinterest, more vacant, absent. Gone.

We lived like nervous little primates around him. We would sit on the sofa or in our big round papa-san chair and watch TV in his presence; or Lisa, Mom, and I would play a game of Bible Trivia at the dining room table—never knowing if something, maybe an episode of *Little House on the Prairie*, would enrage him, jump-start his temper, send us running for cover while Mom tried to calm him down.

He whipped me the night Carter lost to Reagan. "We're losing a good man!" he said with each stroke. "We're losing a Christian man!" It was a chant of moral outrage, although he usually never cared much for religion. A chant, with the belt keeping rhythm.

But I had a sign.

The lacquered sign, proof positive that Rodney was not my father, that our association was accidental or, if anything, a test from God.

The real father of our family was Christ, whose handsome bearded face beamed down from most of our walls. In the hallway, he was the carpenter in simple wool robes, intent on his workbench while an angel watched unseen from the shop's door. In the dining room, over the piano, he was the returning and triumphant king in gold and white, riding a horse through the sky with a sword of truth in his scarred right hand. In my room, he was drawn by an American Indian, and he took on long black-silk hair and high tanned cheekbones—a soft love in his thick brown eyes.

This, I knew, was my defender. This was the father I owned. This was the one who protected me, watched me in my sleep, crowded my room with angels, and stilled the twitching panic in my dreams. This was the one who had proven his love by dying for the world, and who would prove it again on the last day, the day of judgment, when the devil and all of his demons, and Rodney, would be bound and cast forever into the lake of fire. For now, Love held back the thunderclouds of his anger. But in time I would have vindication.

One of the last things my mother ever said to me was, "Pray for Rodney. Pray for him, sweetheart. No one else will."

But I cannot honor that request. He is a patchwork memory, murky shadows of what I want to forget and deny, what I want no longer to be in me or a part of me. He is red hair, plaster dried on ripped blue jeans. Bare-chested anger, beer-sour breath, and nicotine-yellowed hands that shed innocent blood. He is chaos, black-strap reality. And pain.

And there are few prayers left in me.

Mom said once that she met him in a church in North Carolina. In a more honest moment she said it had been a bar. His father was a sharecropper, a tobacco farmer with a few acres and ten or so children to work them. Rodney was born somewhere in the middle of the pack. The redheaded child, he had his father's temper.

I remember his father and remember his family, with their slow, iced-tea accents, their big dogs and tiny trailers, their smells of sweat and fried food and tobacco. And I remember my mother's first couple of dates with Rodney, although I could not have been more than five or six, so they are murky, hazed, and muslin-covered pictures.

He stood in our doorway, wide shouldered and almost handsome in a flannel shirt like a lumberjack's, SKOAL written on his baseball cap in green-and-black lettering. He was still there the next morning, sitting in the kitchen in his cowboy boots and blue jeans, and I thought he wasn't supposed to be there. He said nothing, and my mother was still in bed. So I poured cereal for myself and sat still and ate it quietly; watched him while he bit around an apple core and then squeezed the seeds through his teeth onto the tabletop with a quick wet spit.

And I remember another night that ended with me and my mother outside our house, crouching behind the hedge while he bellowed at her to come back in.

"Don't hit me," she called in to him.

I remember this. There is nothing wrong with this memory.

"I won't hit you if you come inside."

She took my hand in the dark and squeezed. Her fingers were shaking and her nails scratched my skin. She tried to pull, but I didn't want to move.

"It's alright, honey," she said. "You just don't understand."

And that was the trouble with me: I didn't understand. And I never learned to understand. A child's logic, always banging and clattering against her desperation, tugging at her skirt. Ignored.

The third member of the paternal trinity was another shadow, like Jesus. Like Jesus, an agreeable fiction.

My father—my real father—was a black-and-white picture in a frame that I kept hidden away among comic books in a Hefty bag in my closet because Rodney had already smashed it once. He was a picture, a tin box full of pictures, and a name signed to a check that appeared in our mailbox once a month with military regularity.

His absence was natural; his presence, unimaginable. So from his pictures I constructed a dream. A myth. A collage and a lie that became as sure a shelter as the word of God and as guaranteed a salvation as the second coming. He would rescue me.

But he never came.

Superman, the knight from Arthur's court, the messiah with love in his eyes and fury in his hands, never showed. And I waited with a child's faith, the kind of faith that burns only until experience dries up its innocence.

I sat next to her sometimes, on days when the heat rising up from the asphalt streets drove us inside and we locked ourselves in her bedroom and watched the relentless breath of our air conditioner blast frost onto the windows. She would curl up in bed with a religious book or with one of the biographies she loved, while I sat on the floor and drew or read *Le Morte D'Arthur* or *Conan the Conqueror*. Or *Conan the Deliverer*. *Conan the Destroyer*.

And on the best days, I looked up from my world of swords and battles and bloodshed, peered over its edge into our little ice-cold bedroom, and asked her to tell me about him.

And her tales were as rich and as full as anything I was reading, anything I was imagining, better fiction than could be trapped on a black-and-white page. Because, in her stories, she was the princess locked in a tower and he was the knight errant, and I was the prize to be won.

The princess said she had been a prisoner in her parents' house, a tiny captive bundled up in the backseat while her parents scoured Europe for antiques, or trapped like a porcelain statue on a stool in the kitchen while her mother cooked and talked to her about God and sin and a woman's responsibilities. The responsibility to be obedient to her husband, the responsibility to be a good woman, a quiet Christian.

Her parents were Calvinists, Christians who believed that everything is predestined, preordained by God. My grandmother distrusted "modern churches" with their "inexcusable ignorance" of John Calvin. So they attended defective Presbyterian or Baptist churches to keep up appearances but really worshiped at home, studied at home, and sometimes taught my mother, alone, at home.

My mother grew up in disguise. Her father was a linguist in the military during and after the Second World War, and they lived mostly in Germany. In Germany, where she wandered away from their house whenever she thought she might not be missed. In the streets, German and American men worked together, lines of bare backs and flashing shovels. They built new roads, rebuilt bombed-out, ash black buildings. That was why she said, later, that the smell of fresh asphalt always made her think of little girls and handsome men.

But she didn't like American girls, the other American girls. She made only German friends, leaning over their neat white fences, holding out her dolls, until they let her in. Once in, she mirrored them, and they taught her to braid her hair.

Her mother could not learn German; she tried, but it was too hard on the throat, too wet in the back of the throat. She coughed and sputtered and choked on it, and when addressed would smile tightly and say, "Ja, ja, ja," so that no one would guess she could not understand.

My mother knew the Germans' language better than her own. She spoke in German secrets and hated speaking English.

She said that on some nameless day, at some unannounced hour, by the time she was thirteen, it was decided that she was, simply, Not of the Elect. "One of those women," the kind of girl who would always be disobedient, always run after sin. The worst kind of all— the sort who would have a baby before she was married. The kind who would go to hell. Regrettable. Regrettable to be sure. But simple, and preordained.

My mother never tried to explain her mother's divine revelations. Never searched for compassionate reasons behind the words that were poured out all over her like poison. The truth was simple to her, an old truth: her mother hated her. She always had and she always would. That too was preordained.

She met my father by accident, in high school, in 1964, after her family moved back to America, when Vietnam was still something vague and distant—at least to teenagers who were twitching to the British invasion, busy trying to shrug off their definitions, lose their parents, forget the fifties.

Her parents hated him, hated his arrogance, his irreverent humor, hated the goals and dreams he carried as if delivered to him by God on top of Mount Sinai, his future glory chiseled in stone, signed by Jehovah, guaranteed. Hated him most of all for loving their daughter, the one who was divinely unlovable and unlovely.

He was the son of a steelworker, the son of a marine who fought at Iwo Jima. He had his father's blood and pride—enough of it that he too wanted to be a marine. His father had been a Golden Gloves boxer in his teens, and he handed his son that tradition too, gave him the left jab and right cross, the uppercut, taught him to take a fall. So my father took his pride and his wit and mixed them in together. With a poetic love for tight, whitened knuckles and clenched fists.

My mother fought for him, slinking out of her window late at night, escaping from school, becoming an eloquent practitioner of lies. She ran to him to escape the lack of oxygen in her home, the calloused Christianity without a heartbeat. She ran to him to make love in strange places, to leave Jesus and John Calvin on the side of the road shaking their heads sadly, barely visible through the dust of her back wheels.

Perverting years of ballet training, she laid claim to any dance floor, embarrassed my father with splits and back bends and gestures that were probably illegal in the state of Maryland. She told me he danced like a boxer, feet fixed on the linoleum floor, hands in front of his face, while his torso dodged and twitched in a sad attempt at rhythm. She would run her hands over him in time with the backbeat, trying to sculpt a spirit for him, trying to wish silk from cold steel.

She drank and smoked and read forbidden novels. She wrote erotic poetry. In German. She said later that she had *lived*.

Then my mother would imitate my grandmother for effect—half a British accent, and one eyebrow lifted while the rest of her face went dead.

"You're becoming a whore, Michelle. An absolute *whore*."

She said they took her to a chaplain. She sat with her mother and father in his office while the three adults discussed her for an hour. When the Air Force preacher asked her how things were at home, my mother said everything she was supposed to say. She lied with a smile like a proper young lady, ankles crossed and back straight. Recanted and promised to do better. Then she excused herself politely and went into the ladies' room.

In one of the stalls, she smeared out her fragile little truths with a mascara pencil on toilet paper. *Help me. You don't know what it's like. You don't know what she does to me.* On their way out of the office, she secretly slipped the wad of paper to the man's secretary. And never heard from him again.

After high school she followed my father to the naval academy. Midshipmen were forbidden to be alone in a room with a woman, much less marry. And they wanted to marry. He swore that they would marry. And my mother, always a believer, did whatever she had to do, on the strength of that promise—locking herself in the trunk of his friend's car to be smuggled onto the campus, swimming naked in the Annapolis harbor to get his attention.

And somehow, in the shadow of all the prohibitions, in some backseat or secret apartment, in a midshipman's dorm room or maybe in the harbor, I came to be.

She would always say that with the tone of a happy ending. *And then you came.* Then she would go back to her book or tell another story.

It was much later, sometime after those first few weeks with Rodney, that I was sent to live with my grandparents for first and second grades. For safety. I called my grandmother Honey, and Honey too told stories.

But her stories were mixed and mingled in with Bible lessons— God's truth about Noah or Sarah or Abraham intertwined with and no less sacred than Honey's truth about my mother. Early-morning Bible study was as sure as the rising sun, as inevitable.

Gamp made coffee and carried it up to their room on a little white tray, while Honey served up sin. *Our* sins from the previous day.

After the early-morning preachers were finished on the radio, she would scoot up in bed, back straight against the wall, and then judge our words and our deeds under the spotlight of the scriptures and *Institutes of the Christian Religion* by John Calvin. She spread the books out across her white knees. She was thorough, and "harsh," she said. "Harsh because I love you. Now, Scott, you will recall yesterday . . ." There never *was* enough time for Honey to discuss her own sins. I assumed she didn't have any.

And on special days, when the Spirit was upon her, the lessons stretched out backwards through time, and with the husky voice of a revivalist or a reformer she delivered passionate soliloquies on the sins of my parents. She called me into her room, sometimes angrily, sometimes in tears, and I would sit on the floor by her feet.

"Lust," she said. "It was all lust. Your mother was a wonderful little girl, a good Christian girl. Oh, she was so happy back in Germany. But when we moved to the States for her to go to high school, she met . . . him."

That pronoun, when delivered in a certain ominous tone, usually referred to my father.

"Your grandfather and I did everything we could to keep them apart. If we had known then what we know now, we would have killed him. We would have bashed his head in the first time he came around. He sat right out there, right in front of this house, and she would sneak out to meet him. And your poor grandfather never knew what was happening."

I'm hard pressed to remember Honey ever referring to Gamps as anything other than "your poor grandfather." When he sat in on these sessions, he would nod his head approvingly at every turn of the tale, and whenever Honey delivered a woeful "your poor grandfather" line, he never failed to lower his graying head and sigh on cue.

"Then," she would continue, "when *he* went to the naval academy, we thought that would be the last of him. We thought the academy would put a stop to that nonsense. I begged your mother—begged her—to go to finishing school. In Scandinavia. But no, she wanted to ruin her life, she wanted to be with him, she wanted to sin. She had such a promising career as a ballerina, and she just threw it all away, just threw it all to hell and became a nothing. And then, when she got pregnant with you, we thought at least he would marry her so you wouldn't be a b— So you would have a father. But no, of course not, she wasn't *good enough* for him to marry. *Mr. Naval Academy* couldn't resign. *Mr. Naval Academy* had his CAREER to think about!"

And my eyes widened out at the crescendo, stretched out, absorbing a different version of a time I certainly couldn't remember and constructed in childish caricatures like a jigsaw puzzle.

"And then they had the gall to come to us to ask for money for an abortion. An abortion!"

"What's an abortion?"

"An abortion is when a woman goes to the doctor and they kill the baby before it's born. And they wanted your poor grandfather to pay for it. Pay to kill you, because they didn't want you. They said they needed money for something else, but I *knew*—I knew what they were really going to do."

The closing lines were always the same. They produced the requisite tears on the part of all who were participating.

"But we wanted you. We want you now. I love your mother, because God commands us to love our enemies—but she doesn't want you. She wanted to have you aborted. God has given you to us to raise."

And I wiped at my eyes, ashamed of how cruel my parents had been to Honey and my poor grandfather. Ashamed, and then more ashamed still, because no matter how grateful I was that my grandparents wanted me, all I really wanted was to defect, to go home. I was a child and I missed my mother.

Rescue came as a surprise. Toward the end of second grade, Mom showed up and announced to her parents that she had received Jesus as her Savior and was ready to take me home to live with her. Honey and Gamps blocked her in the doorway and reminded her painstakingly that she was then, always had been, and always would be their greatest disappointment and that she had no business raising a child. Mother, a veteran of Honey's Bible studies, agreed wholeheartedly, looked past them, and told me to pack my things.

As we gathered my toys and comic books together, I asked her why she had wanted to have me aborted.

"Who told you that?"

"Honey."

Something dark passed across her face. Then softened out into a smile.

"That's not right," she said matter-of-factly. "She's saying that because she hates me and she wants to get you. She tried to make me give you to them, let them adopt you. That's what really happened. She wanted to take you away from me."

"Don't look at the house, sweetheart," she said as we peeled out of the driveway. Immediately, I pressed my face against the glass to see what she was warning me about. Honey sat at the window in her study on the second floor, staring at us as though she could make the car burst into flames.

She had lost to my mother. Again.

On the road to our new home in Florida, Mom made her second announcement.

"Do you remember Rodney?" she asked, gleaming.

I conjured up a few images, frightening images, and nodded uncertainly.

"Well, guess what," she said, now positively bubbling. "We've gotten married! He's received the Lord, and we've been going to church!"

She pulled the car over and tried to stop my crying.

"Sweetie, he's not so bad," she said, soothing. "He has a little girl. Her name is Lisa. You'll have a little sister."

More crying.

"Did you know that he can put his ear to the ground and tell if a storm is coming? He can—just like an Indian!"

"I don't care."

"And he's received Jesus. He's almost stopped drinking."

We sat on the shoulder of I-95 just north of Daytona, and she began piecing together a new picture of the man I remembered only as the thick, dirty colossus who had thrown us out of our house.

"You need a father," she said.

"I have a father."

"You need a father who's here. One you know. Someone who can teach you things."

"I *have* a father."

"Oh, sweetheart," she said, with something that sounded like pity. "Sweetheart, you don't even remember him."

I remember a box. A black box in a leather case that my mother spoke into. She would sit on her bed, legs crossed like a lotus flower, and record messages to send to my father in Okinawa.

After graduating from the academy, he remembered his promise, and they married. The two walked out of a church under a canopy of swords crossed in the air by other midshipmen. My mother wore a dazzling white wedding gown; he was immaculate in his dress blues.

I was hurried to my grandparents' house, caught up and lost in the day's confusion. Toys and books in an overnight bag, nervous voices, angry people. I don't know which of these pictures are hers and which are mine; I was only three. But I think that Honey and Gamp drove me to a park that day, while my mother disappeared in her white dress in a car with someone I didn't recognize. I wanted to feed the ducks at the park, so bits of wheat bread were given to me, and I held them out nervously to birds that were half my size, as they snapped greedily and painfully at my fingertips. I didn't know that I was being hidden from the academy. I didn't know, running from the goddamned ducks, that I was a source of shame, a dirty secret, and I would have been too young to care.

My father, I guess, was too old to care. The secret didn't weigh enough to hold him down. He *did* care about seeing combat in Vietnam—he could smell the mortar fire ten thousand miles away, and something drew him toward it, something in his bloodstream. He wanted to see action, he wanted to lead, he wanted a patriotic reason to use his fists. He asked for the front line.

The corps promptly stationed him in Okinawa, stranding him agonizingly close to the action, helpless and powerless as the death notices of the academy's best and brightest came across the wires day after motionless day.

So my mother sent him tapes, recordings of her voice, to keep him company, to keep him strong and sane. She cried about her loneliness, asked him when he was coming home, as if he knew, as if he had any choice, as if he wanted to come home. She was his youth on a cassette tape—she even called him Corky, his childhood nickname. Somewhere I still have one of those tapes. There is my mother's voice, sounding too young, too fresh, saying, "Say hello, sweetheart."

And there I am, four-year-old mouth still struggling around syllables and *r*'s: "Hello, Cowky."

"No, honey, not Corky. Daddy. *Dad-dy*. Say hello to Daddy."

"Hello, Cowky."

And then silence, and some frustration, and the sharp *click!* of the recorder being shut off, so Mom could explain the concept of "Daddy" to me.

And at some point during his absence, she began losing her fight to love him. For five years she had been pulling muscles sneaking out of windows, carrying her baby around Annapolis like a time bomb, filling the air with lies. But when he was gone, when he was so far gone that none of her devices or smiles, none of her anger or passion, could stop a war and bring him close enough to touch again, she made a gentle pirouette away.

The recorded messages became infrequent, detached, full of the talk one makes with old friends instead of young lovers. She found lovers in other men. When my father came home at last, she asked for a divorce. They were both too tired for fighting.

So my father did not exist. He was less a part of reality than Big Bird or Donald Duck or God. He was a name, a strange name, "Corky," neatly contained in a little black box, whispered by adults in my presence as if it somehow concerned me.

Jimmy was real.

Jimmy was 1968—long hair, love beads, and bandannas—alive and well and in love with my mother in 1973. The three of us would drive to the beach and rent a tiny wooden house for a weekend or sometimes a full week.

Jimmy stretched out on a huge tie-dyed blanket with my mother, and they talked about things that sailed over my head like seagulls, things that made my mother blush and throw back her head and laugh. He built sand castles as tall as I was, would crouch behind them, peer through the crude towers, shooting at me with his fingers.

He played like that for hours, I guess loving the way my mother loved him for it.

Then sometimes Jimmy would disappear. Nothing much was said about his absences at the time, but years later, on those rare days when my mother would speak about him, she would mumble something about his "trouble with the law." I don't know what Jimmy did for a living. A few possibilities spring to mind.

It had been days, maybe a week, since we had seen him, so my mother and I drove to the apartment where he was living with friends. I waited in her brown Ford Maverick, listening to B. J. Thomas on an eight-track and checking every few minutes to make sure the doors to the car were locked.

What would you give to silence your memories? To take them out of the present tense?

She runs out of the apartment complex, her hands up in the air, waving in front of her face; stumbling and running in a way that sends fear crawling up from my groin, electrocution in the stomach. She fights with the car door. *"I am trying,"* I say from inside, *"I am trying to unlock the door,"* but she cannot hear my muffled voice. She slaps the window again and again, pounding on the tinny roof with the palms of her hands, and then she is in.

"It's the judgment of God, it's the judgment of God," she screams. She looks around herself, at the car seat, at me, looking for something new to say, looking as if she has lost something, grinding the engine, starting the car.

"It's the judgment of God!"

"What's wrong, Mommy? What's wrong?"

"Jimmy!" And I learn how much pain can go into a word. Jimmy! and the fear reaches my ears and my eyes. Jimmy! and I am crying, feeling like a stranger locked outside myself, some older boy, some older thing inside, afraid, who cannot let me in.

"Mommy, where's Jimmy?"

She swerves the car toward a curb and cuts the motor. B. J. Thomas is still playing, the dashboard lights are on, there is too much sound. She pounds on the steering wheel, hitting it like an enemy, hitting it again and again, kicking at the clutch and brakes until I think her legs will snap.

"He's dead! O Jesus, forgive me, he's dead."

"He bought this for me—he was buying this for me," she says, clutching at a gold chain around her neck, smiling in a way that is wrong and frightening. "He had it on layaway. His father . . . O Jesus! . . . his father paid for it, his father gave it to me."

"Is Jimmy coming back?" I ask.

"No, sweetheart, he isn't. He isn't. Jimmy is dead. And it's Mommy's fault."

"Why, Mommy? Why? Why is it your fault?"

"Because Mommy made God angry."

Jimmy went out for a boat ride. He had some drinks, he slipped, I still don't understand. Jimmy just went out for a boat ride and he never came back. And God never stopped being angry at my mother.

We'll all be sleeping in our own beds tonight.

Mom came down with a bad flu, and Rodney volunteered to go to Albertsons drugstore to get her some fresh soup. He's been gone now for three days. Things have been quiet, Mom's feeling better anyway, and the soup has turned to Jell-O by now, wherever it may be.

Night again. I've become a nocturnal creature like my sister and mother. Sleep is something one struggles to achieve. Thoughts bounce lightly around the room, hitting against the picture of Christ and the poster of Superman, and sometimes they float up to God.

Lord God, I confess that I am a sinner, unworthy of your blood and grace. Forgive me all my sins for the sake of . . . what's next?

Hell's next, boy. Hell is closer than you think . . .

Forgive me all my sins for the sake of your son, Jesus. Jesus. Jesus, I think there's something wrong with me.

Men crowd my dreams. Unwelcome tormentors, they vie and struggle with each other for attention, elbowing out all prayers and all resistance, a hormonal jihad for control.

The devil's gone shopping tonight. And it's my soul that he's after.

I want.

Lord God, my soul is marred by sin.
When I grow up . . .
I confess that I am a sinner.
I want to marry a man.
A most shameful and vile sinner.
I don't know why. When I grow up . . .
Unworthy of your forgiveness, alienated from your grace.
I want to marry a man.
I confess . . .

I hear small sounds, coming, I guess, from the kitchen. Leaving God in my room, I creep warily down the narrow hallway. It is littered with bits of paper that stick to the bare bottoms of my feet.

She is sitting in the kitchen with the gray tin, her box of memories. Scattered around her chair are photographs in various stages of dismemberment. Strangers' arms and legs and torsos, half a head of someone I think I recognize.

"What are you doing?"

"Housecleaning," she says with an Auschwitz smile.

On the table, she has neatly lined up ten or more faces—the faces of a little girl grinning up with black-and-white braces and German braids. All of the other pictures have been dissected meticulously with scissors, but these, these have been specially chosen. These have been torn apart by hand.

There is something here. The demons in my room are hollow and mute compared to these. The little girl. Her eyes. My mother's eyes. The same eyes, twenty-two of them in this dark room, and I can only choke out a single question.

"Are those pictures of my father?"

"Some of them . . ." She stops and sets down her scissors, looks up as though some terrible revelation, some dark angel, has just fluttered into the room.

"Sweetheart, I'm so sorry. I'm sorry. I should have asked you. Did you want them?"

I take the tin box, cradling it under one arm.

"Yes, I want them."

Of course I want them. If you don't want them anymore, then they are mine. They belong to me.

• • •

It was a dark day when the sodomites came, when the homosexuals invaded our neighborhood.

"Goddamn faggots." Rodney said it as though it were a question, standing shirtless by the living room window. "Goddamn faggots moving in."

"You're kidding," my mother said and ran over next to him. "O sweet Lord! I've got to call Pastor."

They had looked like ordinary people, pulling up in their old, beat-up car; one of them carried in a box of tools, and he wore a mechanic's jumpsuit. We overheard them talking. Reassuring deep-throated Southern accents. They sounded like good people. If it weren't for the kiss, we might never have known.

But then the other one, the bigger man with the mustache, squeezed by his roommate at their front door, and Rodney said he saw him touch him on his ass, kiss the other man's neck. Then they looked around quickly. Guilty. Rodney darted behind the curtain; it was the only time I ever saw him afraid.

"You are not to go outside," my mother said to me. "Not under any circumstances, unless you tell me. You can go in the backyard if you want to play."

They came in the beginning of the summer, and for the next three months I went to the backyard to play.

Mother called it Mission Impossible—our plan to convert them. We drove to the gospel bookstore in the mall and bought a stack of Christian tracts, tiny booklets that described hell and told you how to get into heaven.

"You wait," she said. "Go stand by their car and look casual. If the window is open, then nod once. Then wait until I give you the signal. If the coast is clear, throw the tract in, and get back here as quick as you can."

After a successful mission we hid in my room, peering out through the shutter until one of them came out. The smaller man would sit sometimes in the car and read them. And we would join hands and thank Jesus for that. The bigger man tore them up or threw them on the street. They would be in his car again the next day, whole or in fragments. That summer we filled their front seat with books and Gideon Bibles again and again and again.

Our backyard was small, so I moved out into the alley. The alleyway ran the length of our block and was almost as wide as a street. It was thick with tropical bushes and tall weeds, and I could pretend it was a jungle full of metal trash bins.

Beside some stranger's bin I found the box.

It was full of wigs, elaborate and ornamental. George Washington wigs and wigs for Cleopatra. Half-empty jars and cases of brown or peach makeup. And old fabric, solid black or brilliant colors, some with oriental designs.

I may as well have discovered the Ark of the Covenant.

Dragging it back to the house, I scooted it into the garage and tried the costumes on in front of an old chipped full-length mirror. Wound the cloth around my chest and waist and became a Roman soldier. Put on the dark wig with the long bangs and looked a little like a woman. Another wig and a heavy cloak, and I was the Son of Man.

I hid the box in a corner behind the toolshed, wedged beside the water pump, but kept the wigs aside. My mother was in her room taking a nap; the air conditioner hummed and rattled in her window, and it was too hot for her not to be asleep. So I hooked the long green waterhose up to the pump and started washing the piles of hair, rinsing out the age and the dust, looking over my shoulder. When they were clean I lined them up neatly in a long row on the pavement of the driveway, left them out in the sun to dry.

Less than an hour later, I heard my mother scream.

"Evelyn! Evelyyyyyyyn!" She was hanging out of her bedroom window, screaming for our neighbor. "Evelyn, come quickly! The homosexuals! The homosexuals!"

Evelyn came running and met her in the driveway.

"What is it? What is it?"

"I don't know!" Mother was hysterical, crying. "I just looked outside and they were here! They must have come while I was sleeping!"

Then she looked at me, and a whole new wave of emotions crashed. She grabbed me, held me against her chest until I could not breathe.

"And little Scottie was playing right here in the backyard! O my God, my God, they could have gotten him!"

Evelyn picked up a broken palm frond and nudged at the lumps as if they were time bombs.

"Look at them, Michelle," she said. "They're all wet."

"They've sprayed them with chemicals or urine or something."

"I'm calling the police!" Evelyn said. "So help me God, I'm calling the police!"

"They won't do anything. We didn't see them. They're too smart for that."

"Then we're giving them back. Scott, go inside."

I watched from my bedroom while the two women picked up sticks and carefully lifted my wigs up off the ground. They carried them out into the middle of the street and then hurled them, spinning in the air, onto the faggots' lawn.

When there was only one left, Mom carried it all the way across the street.

"Michelle!" Evelyn called. "Michelle, get back here! What are you doing?"

She walked up to their front door, took the wig off the end of her stick, and draped it over the doorknob. She walked back quickly, almost running, wiping her hands on her dress.

"They're the ones attacking," she said. "We've got to fight back."

When the big man came home that night he only paused for a second when he got out of his car. Then he walked slowly, shoulders tight, eyes straight forward, into his house. The smaller man came out later and picked up the wigs with rubber gloves.

They came home with a dog the next day. A rottweiler with a studded collar and thick black bones and muscles.

"You know why they did that," my mother said. "So they could have sex with it."

"People don't do that," I said. "They don't really do that, do they?"

"*They* do. They're not people."

And I was glad. I was so relieved to learn that they were not people.

Mom forgot all about the tracts after what was forever known as the Wig Incident. Instead, we littered their lawn. Whole bags of garbage on their doorsteps or on the hood of their car. Some nights we stayed up late watching, shadowed on the front porch. Then we crept out and made our point, made our statement.

"They're filthy," my mother said. "Like animals. Full of demons."

Evelyn found a condom in her alley. Used and full and yellowed. That too ended up on their door.

Within two weeks they were gone.

Mom feels better sometimes when she hits Lisa.

Sometimes there is this something in the air between them, this cold steel something, and Mom has a look on her face as if she's walking around on broken glass. Lisa hides in her room because she knows what is coming, she hides in her room and reads Catherine Marshall or Nancy Drew books.

And Mom stands in the kitchen with her arms folded, worrying, before she calls Lisa in and tells her to do something constructive. So Lisa comes in in her day dress, with her hair pulled back sharply into a clean ponytail so that her face is taut and her eyes are lifted around the corners. She has to wear her hair this way because girls have to be clean and pretty, and Mom says it makes her look like a china doll, so it is worth having headaches.

"Wait a minute. Wait—a—minute," Mom says. "Before we even begin. Wipe that arrogance off your face right now, young lady."

"Yes, ma'am."

"Here, peel these." And she gives her a blue Tupperware bowl of potatoes. The rest of them are in the pan already, hissing.

I usually think my mother is pretty.

"You think I don't know," she says to Lisa's back. "You think I don't know what you're thinking, but I do."

"Yes, ma'am."

But sometimes she is ugly.

"What was that?"

"Yes, ma'am."

"Oh, you're just so put upon, aren't you? Poor Lisa. Daddy's little baby."

Sometimes she acts like a man.

"Yes, ma'am."

Mom lunges at her, takes her by the ponytail, and leads her to the sink.

"You're going to grow up to be a whore if you're not careful, do you hear me? Girls like you get pregnant before they're married."

"That's not true," Lisa says. It is only a statement. It is only a statement because Lisa does not cry. Lisa says things. Lisa can turn into stone.

"You're calling me a liar? Open your mouth," my mother says. "OPEN YOUR MOUTH!"

Mom takes the Palmolive liquid detergent and pulls Lisa's head back. She talks to her while she pours in the green soap.

"I'm going to pray for you, Lisa. I'm going to pray that God sends you an old man. An old man who will be good to you and will keep you from being a tramp."

Lisa is struggling, and the air and the spit make green bubbles around the corners of her mouth. Mom holds her tightly. Mom is crying.

"You won't care if he's old, because you like being Daddy's little girl, don't you? Don't you?"

More of the green.

"Close your mouth, Lisa. Close your mouth. Good. Good girl. Now swallow."

The next day, Mother is full of I-love-yous and presents. Little wax candles in the shape of horses and puppies. Yellow dresses and dolls.

Lisa takes the dolls and combs their hair and polishes their eyes and sets them on a high shelf above her dresser. I take them down and tease her with them sometimes. But Lisa does not play with dolls. Lisa does not care.

two

There are places where the earth whispers to you.

There are places where the ground speaks, maybe the dust of the dead. Maybe the memories of those who long ago turned to dust, murmuring upward in Gregorian rhythm, gentle echoes whispering through the soles of your feet.

And in those places, you *know*. You know the answers or you know the warnings. You know when to speak and when to remain silent. *Hush, child, there is danger here. Hush, child, do not breathe.* You will know when to hide.

I lived in such a place. And we were fragile shadows who learned not to speak, mute little birds who never shouted when we were angry and never cried ourselves to sleep. To shout or cry was an admission that something, *anything*, was wrong; and nothing was wrong, of course. Nothing *could* be wrong in a world where God is standing behind every closed door and scriptures are timeless outlines spoken in time and angels dance unseen in living rooms and alleyways, beside the backyard fence, living, twirling, guiding, even in the spaces between our tiny fingers.

Then there are times when the earth just sounds like dirt.

I was thirteen when the earth sounded just like dirt.

• • •

He drove a truck, a Ford truck with a big silver ram's head on the hood and tires that lifted it high above the ground, the king in his carriage. On quiet nights, nights that would be quiet, it floated into the driveway with the engine cut and the lights dimmed. On other nights it roared and burned and squealed like an injured rabbit.

Lisa and I knew its sounds. We lay awake in our beds and tuned and strung up our ears like instruments to listen for the tires churning against the concrete that ran the length of our house. And we sensed, we *felt*, the tread of rubber on our ears and predicted the night. Bruise and belt and motion.

That night there were hot rubber sounds that stung and then echoed. And then he lay on the horn for a while, underscoring his message, an auditory exclamation point. So we waited for the next measure. Next there would be voices. We waited for voices. Voices through the drywall, muffled tones running high or low—more evidence that would tell us whether we should try to sleep, heads under the covers to fool him if he looked in, or if we should go to the closets.

I remember that the grass was wet from an afternoon rain, so it must have been in fall, and skies were darker and wet with gray, which meant night was coming fast, so I suppose that means November.

It was November. And Mother went out to meet him.

Yelling from the front lawn. Lisa and I ran to my bedroom window and watched. Mother stood on one side of the truck, clutching the steel rim of the flatbed, and Rodney was on the other side, darting to the left and to the right, and as he would move in one direction, she would move to the other, the two circling the truck like predator and prey in an after-school documentary. It was the Road Runner and Wile E. Coyote, and they made us laugh.

So we went outside to watch in the light that was fading. Stood a few yards from the front porch with our backs to the street and a route of escape. And neighbors came out on their porches.

Embarrassed.

Embarrassed by the attention, Rodney ran faster around the truck, stumbling and sliding on the concrete, becoming angrier, maybe sobering, but coming after her faster and faster until she tried to cut away across the lawn. But then he lunged, caught her by her thighs, brought her down.

God is always angry with my mother.

And who needs a belt when you have your boots? When you have your brand-new boots from Swayze's Western Men's Apparel? Boots for the urban cowboy, boots like *real* men wear, brown etched leather and steel tips. He stood and kicked her. He did it once and then again, this time with a different slant, calculating the curve of his hip like an artist or an athlete—carefully—evaluating his performance.

Her long hair fell out of its neat pins, spilled on the grass, and her back is arching towards me, ballooning out, deflating around his leg like a busted soccer ball.

Lisa is gone. She is hiding. But my legs are concrete, I cannot move; my brain is crooked, and everything is twisting from adrenaline, everything is surreal.

There is another audible thud against her body, and then her leg shoots up into his groin. He stumbles backward, and she crawls away from him with white shock on her face—as if she had forgotten that she had been strong once; forgotten that in another life she had been a dancer.

And someone is yelling from across the street, you son of a bitch.

"I'm calling the police, you son of a bitch!"

And he is kicking her again.

"Leave her alone. I said I'm calling the cops!"

More kicking, and a new voice chiming in, "Come after me, you motherfucker! Why don't you come after me?"

My voice. Words I have learned from him, his only gift, his only legacy to me—the sound of anger, the language of rage. There is depth in me I did not know, there is rage in me, bitter synonym of strength.

"You cocksucking motherfucker! Come get me!"

He stops and looks, stunned, shocked at the obscenities, taken off guard. Mother moves away, but he kicks her again, torn between preventing her escape or putting his hands on my throat.

"You're a motherfucker," I howl.

"You're a son of a bitch," he says.

"You—fuck—your—*mother!*" I hold out my arms, "Come and get me," and that is enough for him, the decision is made. He comes. I walk backwards, pacing, timing this, giving her room, giving her room to run, and she does get up, but she is walking in the wrong direction, she is walking back toward the truck, toward the flatbed.

"Motherfucking little son of a bitch," he growls and grows larger, but all I can think is *what is she doing*, reaching down into the flatbed, picking something up, coming up behind him.

"Son of a—"

There is a whistling sound that fills the air, and a dark thud, and Rodney is down, clutching an arm, bouncing back up and backing away from my mother, who is swinging a length of pipe over her head like a helicopter blade, some primal sound caught in her clenched teeth, swinging this lead pipe, and the bastard is running.

He makes it to his truck, leaps in, and locks the doors.

"You're crazy!" I hear him screaming at her through the glass, but now his voice is muffled, baffled. She brings the pipe down hard on the hood of his truck, again and again, two or three times, before he has the keys in the ignition and peels out onto the street in reverse.

He did not come home that night or for many nights afterwards. Mother waited for him with her makeup on and her hair down around the shoulders of her new nightgown.

She knew that Rodney had a girlfriend, because she had asked him and he had said yes. He kept saying yes, and she kept asking him. So a little past midnight, after spending another evening on the porch in her rocking chair, she would drive us, and drive us too fast, to the strange woman's apartment complex. Dim her lights and shush us, just circling, just making sure that the silver ram truck was parked there.

We knew that he would come home. No doubt and no question. And Mother wanted him to come home, although I did not know why. She wanted him back in his chair. And she began to say that she feared for me, feared for my soul and my salvation, because I had sinned when I had screamed out those words in rage.

So I was sent to my grandparents' house, I was sent away, because she feared for my soul, because she was afraid for my life.

When he came home, he beat her. Beat her badly. Then said he wanted a divorce. And she cried because she was losing him.

That summer at my grandparents', I was on restriction. I don't remember why, exactly—maybe a careless word or some minor act of irresponsibility. A little excuse, a little sin; a little justification for Honey to punish her daughter.

Bullshit. Theory. Armchair psychiatry.

Still, the words were spoken: "You're just like your mother."

I learned I was becoming just like my mother. Something in my tone, she said, something in the facial expressions.

"Arrogance!"

Arrogant and becoming just like her, just like the "bad seed"; and just as for her, hell's gates were groaning open already to receive me. You can hear them if you listen closely.

Repent. Repent.

"Quickly, before it's too late."

And so that was why I was on restriction. To remind me of hell.

But restriction was not hell. It was just quiet.

And in that quiet mercy, old thoughts that had loitered next to me since earliest childhood stood up and grew vivid and swelled in the silent little room with the creaking floorboards. Loud and embarrassing. Jesus was watching. Jesus is always watching.

"If any boy ever does this to you . . ." Where did those words come from? My mother sitting on her bed, holding a glossy picture in a bent-back magazine.

"If any boy ever does this to you, you come and tell me right away!" I see the sketch of an older boy kneeling in front of a slightly younger boy, hands groping inside his blue jeans. It's a Christian magazine, one of God's publications. Mother's face is serious and grim.

"This is called a child molester," she said. "They hide in the woods and grab other little boys and play with them."

She paused, looked around the room.

"*Down there*," she whispered, pointing to her lap. "Play with them *down there*."

It must have been 1978, because I was still riding my 1976 Bi-centennial bicycle with the red-white-and-blue stripes and stars and the flaming tassels on the handlebars. Ten years old, maybe fifth grade. And every day thereafter I leapt on my bike after school and rode far out on the dirt roads around our house. Past the junkyard, past civilization, until there were only dark and green woods on either side of the road. And then stopped my bike, heart pounding, stood there straddling it, bouncing it back and forth between my legs, waiting and hoping for one of those welcomed monsters to come out of the woods and play with me . . . *down there.*

He never came.

Except at night. At night he always came. And came as he had always come, slinking through a window into my dreams, brilliant and brown haired and much older—old enough to be in the sixth or seventh grade, even—and he would talk to me and put his arms around me and smile through strong white teeth. A devilish grin, a tinderbox full of glossy, unknown things.

He changed over the years, grew up with me. One imaginary friend among many childish illusions, but with more power. Power for moving reality, shifting the orbits of stars, at least internally. Power that made me shiver to think of him, stretch and ache with excitement, high-voltage electric itching in the skin whenever I called him into being, whenever I gave him a name.

Memories are my trade, and I cloister with them, guard them, sleep on them like gold. Even these, even the ones that have the dark sparkle to them, purple beneath diamond, sweet and bruised and in pain.

Pain grew into certainty, certainty blossomed out confusion, and confusion erupted again into pain. A full circle, all the seasons, wrapped up in, nourished by, and summed up in shame. Does that make sense? It didn't then.

But I could remember even then that once my thoughts had been my own. Givens. Before they told me that I was a sinner, before they told me that God is always watching and you are always wrong. Before all that, the words and pictures in my mind had been the most secret and natural features in the world, pure and undefiled, crystalline and comforting and contrasted with the world of the adults that was always and invariably this great gulping monster with an insatiable appetite and me on his mind.

First grade? Christ, how the shadows extend through time.

Adults talked to us then as though we were imbeciles, with clinking melodies in their voices and feigned interest in everything from our miserable long school days to our bodily functions. They loved to ask us questions they knew we could not answer, and taught with the smug adult conviction that we lacked all power to question. Childhood, the monologue.

"Is there anyone special in your class?" That loaded question was once posed to me. "Is there anyone you like especially?"

Easy enough.

"Allan," I chirped, and smiled a little at their laughter.

"I mean, is there anyone you think is pretty?" my grandmother rephrased the question.

"I think Allan is pretty."

"No." And there was suddenly a tinge of irritation in her voice. "I mean, is there anyone you might want to grow up and marry?"

"Allan," I said again, and welcome to hell, kid. We have experience with the likes of you.

"Boys do not like boys in that way. Boys who like boys in that way are perverts. And perverts do not go to heaven when they die."

So I just walked inside. I walked inside myself to that place where a million other boys like me have gone, to reinvent ourselves and commence growing up silently. Went inside, closed the door, began hiding, began fading, began trying to fit that label, "pervert," on myself, trying it on like a parochial school uniform that scratched and itched and I hated it.

Christ, I knew nothing about sex. Sex was not on the curriculum in our school, it was not included in the flannel-board Bible lessons, it was certainly not dinnertime conversation, and it had nothing to do with Allan. My body was still a bathtub mystery, a curved and peach-colored Rubik's Cube, safe and clean and cloaked in the same prohibitions every child learns and accepts until his hormones dictate differently. All I knew was that I liked Allan, thought he was pretty, liked his smile and the way he talked, liked everything about him in a way that I didn't like any other boy or girl, and if I had to get married someday, why not to him? Liked him in a way that made me shy around him, shy and jealous of his friends.

I liked him, and liking him was wrong. And when I was invited to his birthday party, I pretended that it was a special invitation instead of the generic invitation to the whole class. I pretended and begged to go and cried when I couldn't take the card I had made for him myself, with the big red heart in the center and stars and purple spaceships around the corners. I sneaked it to the party anyway and remember the embarrassment when he looked at it with his puzzled face scrunched up, and his mother said something along the lines of, Allan, be nice.

Be nice, and say thank you.

He did, but he didn't really want to. He must have known I was a pervert. Later, on the playground, I beat the hell out of him, and his mother drove me home.

In grammar school we were all good Christian boys. We started each day with a prayer, sitting on hard wooden pews in chapel, watching our pastor walk to the pulpit, a big black Bible under his arm, Thor carrying thunder, hearing its familiar thud on the lectern, the slow turning of gold-leafed pages, all amplified, all full of scratches and whistling through a worn-out speaker system.

And when we prayed, it was to the God who hovered above us in the air, ever present, ever seeing, eavesdropping on our stolen conversations, reading our minds and projecting our thoughts, they told us, onto a video screen in heaven for Jesus and the angels to see.

We all knew that our lives and our souls were on constant display, each boy visualizing a unique heaven where he was the primary focus, *he* was the particular sinner who ate up God's time listening to tortured prayers of contrition, *he* was the one who made angels weep, and *he* was the one who made Jesus cover up his face with strong, nail-scarred hands, made him cover his face for shame.

There was nothing that was pure and nothing left sacred. Not our words, not our actions, not our thoughts—it was all one long rape, all the boys, the boys who liked boys and the boys who liked girls, we were all bent over the altar of that facade of Christianity, spread-eagled and sacrificed by self-righteous men who pretended that the temples of their minds had never been corrupted by anything more than a passing, fleeting sexual thought.

And we believed what we were told to believe, whether it was a belief about God or a belief about men. The line separating the two was wax-paper thin. We looked at the pastors and teachers as if they were demigods, as if their feet never touched the cheap red carpeting that covered the floors of the sanctuary, as if they were somehow above and beyond sin, monoliths of righteousness, walking radio towers tuned into the Trinity, with the keys to heaven for those who believed them and passports to hell for those who had the audacity to doubt.

And I was the first to worship at their shrines, to fall in homage before their shadows, waiting desperately for the word or the sermon or the Bible memory verse that could free me from the demons that made me different. I was the first to raise my hand to answer a question the right way—the way we had been taught to answer. I was the first of those who announced we had been "called by God" to be ministers, to follow in the footsteps of those who held out the promises of salvation and damnation. I was the first to have a contrite heart and the first to beat my fists against my head, crying for redemption, crying out that I deserved Christ's holy condemnation.

I was the chief of sinners. I was the most defiled. The other boys were amateurs at guilt and self-loathing. Because, I was sure, they were at least normal. Their sins made sense to God, they were predictable and generic, while mine threw him into confusion, the throngs of heaven whispering frantically to one another, putting down their harps to gossip about me on the corners of the streets of gold.

I reached out to the God who threatened to damn me, late at night when the feelings grew strong and I could still see the junior high boys with their shirts off, tied like Gypsies' scarves around their necks or around their waists, playing basketball on the asphalt lot, sweating and laughing and smiling and cursing under their breath. I reached out to God and asked him to take it all away or kill me, let me die but let me enter heaven. Let me be like them, undefiled. Pure.

God was silent. So silent I thought that he must hate me. I knew that he must hate me. And knew that he was justified.

And still, for all the searching, the praying, the discipline and fear that far outstretched my child's body, far outstressed the circuitry in my growing brain, still for all that and in spite of that and in guilt-filled defiance of that, I loved.

And my loves were quiet, secret tender flowers that I crushed from time to time.

Or is that just the way I wish I could have been?

Everyone knew that David was a faggot.

He walked like a woman, with a sway in his round hips that marked him eternally for persecution; he was creative and flamboyant, at least around his girlfriends—although he was quiet and shy around the boys—and worse still, he sang in the school choir. He sang soprano in the school choir.

We all hated him instinctively. No, then again, it wasn't instinctive. The male teachers in our school hated him, our PE coach rolled his eyes and lisped around him, our pastor avoided him *and* his family as if they were space invaders with furry antennas poking out of their heads. Come to think of it, I think that his family hated him too—at least, they never sat with him in church, as if to make the silent statement: hey, everybody, he's not with *us*.

But no one hated David more, no one loathed him more, no one became more irritated with the gossipy talk he made with the girls or the way he never could hiss out his *s*'s without them failing in a spitty *th*, and no one caused more pain in his life than me.

"Know how you can tell a fag?" the perennial, eternal, timeless locker-room conversations would begin.

"His fly's in back?"

"No, man, he's the first one in the showers and the last one out. Hahahahahahahaha!"

"You mean like David?" I would chime in, sharing the laughter and oh so very relieved when they would say, "Yeah, like Davie, har, har, har," instead of, as in my deepest and darkest nightmares, turning in unison and shouting, "No, asshole. We mean *like you!*" and then rolling around on the floor, clutching their sides with laughter.

It was all very clear. David was a faggot, aka a pansy. I, on the other hand, was a man. A real man. I played first string on the football team—granted, only on the line—but the point was that I was no fairy. David was the fairy. I was going through some kind of phase. In fact, I bet that *all* the guys were really going through the same phase, they were all just pretending to like women. Maybe that's how it works, maybe you pretend to like women until one morning you wake up and can't wait to get at Marsha Parker.

Then one day David made the mistake of trying out for the football team, and my entire little version of the universe was thrown into question.

"Daa-vie," the other boys taunted him, bending their wrists and pointing their pinkies skyward. "Daaaa-vie, betcha can't wait to get on a pair of tights."

I just stood there, shaking my helmeted head in sad disbelief. Why the hell would he do this to himself? What could he possibly have been thinking? Didn't he realize he was invading the territory of us real men? Did his father make him do this? Had the man no mercy?

We lined up and, after a prayer, began our training routine. Our lives were on the line here. Next year was the eighth-grade banquet, and the simple rule was: no jersey, no date. So we all played hard and rejoiced at the opportunity to knock David around the muddy field without the coach's intervention or the slightest fear of sustaining an after-school detention.

Finally practice came to an end, and we sat down to hear the coach's decision.

"Well, you all made it," he said, sighing.

And then we looked around, counted ourselves, and realized that we had the minimum number of boys needed to be in the league. Every boy in junior high had shown up, and coach had no option. We were all on the team, all of the boys. All of the boys and David.

That was a sad and bitter day. In the locker room we undressed and fumed, David off in a corner where he had long ago learned to keep to himself, and the rest of us staring at him and decrying the injustice of the situation.

"You know you never would have made the team if we'd had any more guys."

David tuned out, playing deaf.

"You know that, don't you? You know that, right?"

• • •

A few days later I passed him in the hallway. He was walking by himself and it was after school, when even most of the teachers had gone home. He was walking, swaggering by himself with a stack of board games, Bible Trivia and Monopoly and Payday, under his arm.

I think I snapped when he smiled at me.

My fist hit his jaw hard, snapping it shut and cracking my knuckles. That was all it took, and he was sitting down on the floor with his eyes opened wide; and a hundred little game pieces, orange fortune cards, and yellow, blue, and green money spilled and fluttered down the hallway. I turned around and ran.

A few days later, standing in line for lunch, I whispered to him: "So why didn't you turn me in?"

"I dunno."

"Yeah, well."

Jesus was watching.

"Yeah, well," I said. "I'm sorry." And I don't remember ever speaking to him again.

And it wasn't the last time I used my fists or my words to hurt someone. It wasn't the last time I pounded out my pain and my secret and my denial, pounding it into the bodies of boys or men who, in a perfect world, a world without people like me, would have been my brothers. Could have been my friends. Or my lovers, if they would have had me.

And if all these memories are tiny shards of glass, if each one is its own private looking glass, cruel or kind, sucking me in and down with its own small center of gravity . . . then I want to brush my hands through the fragments and find something, some one piece that is not so bittersweet, that is not so much like mulled wine, bitter before it is sweet and bitter after.

It could not all have been only darkness. I want to find something brilliant, something without anger, a memory that transcends the void and stands alone in sharp relief, conducting light instead of eating it.

• • •

It was a brilliant day, too cool for August, the day she handed me
my history, ladling it in the palms of her hands as if scooped from
a holy fountain, pouring it out over me and into me, the sweet balm
of Gilead, sweet healing for old questions and unanswered wounds.

She appeared mid-August, the day before my fourteenth birthday,
at the end of the summer of restriction. She told her parents that
we would be leaving. They met her with coldness and condemnation,
no surprise, but she shrugged them off, a half smile her new defense,
and it kept them at bay.

I wanted nothing for my birthday except to go home. To leave
with her and start the life without Rodney that still, after a summer
of dreaming, was a vague improbability. But she said that we would
stay another day, so I waited with a beggar's patience.

She woke me in the morning. Told me to get dressed. Then we
walked out to the car, leaving Lisa and the family asleep inside, and
stole along winding roads and shortcuts to Annapolis. She pointed
to things, to buildings and places and fields, and gave them all
meaning.

"That's the high school where I met your father. He was shy.
You are like him. He was very shy . . ."

"That used to be a bar, where we would dance. Where your father
would try to dance . . ."

Stories paved the road until we reached the red-brick streets of
the tiny city, the churches with their French spires in miniature,
the apartments scrunched too close to sidewalks, the sound of water
from the harbor.

We spent that day in stores and coffee shops, walking past the
apartment where she had been hidden, swelled and fat with me; past
the church where they were married, walking beneath the canopy
of midshipmen's crossed swords; around the grounds of the naval
academy, a place I knew from pictures in my box. She wove her
tapestry, rich and engrossing, while I asked questions and soaked in
the texture of the water, the rocks, freeze-framing them all into an
order and a sequence.

She told me about their love and about their fights. Showed me
a hill where they had had an argument and he had turned on his

heel and walked away from her, and she had chased him, caught him by his raincoat, almost pulled him down. She told me about their secrecy and about their lovemaking, frantic and desperate and full of mercy. And she said it all without self-censure, without thought of hell or heaven or her parents or her husband or her Savior.

And it all became a prayer. Incorporated in that place without words. But if I had to give those feelings words and I had to draw a close or a meaning to that one day, that one fragile memory, it would only be to say to God, or the gods, or whoever it is that plays dice with the universe: Thank you. I thank you that I came from love.

It was Bill who taught me how to speak. He didn't mean to. It was an accident.

We met by accident in the fourth grade, where we were the tallest and the biggest and the most afraid of God. We were too tall for the fourth grade and were always running into things. And the school photographer who showed up once a year stood us on the back row, behind everyone else, on boxes behind the bleachers. That's how we met. By accident. Bumping against each other in the back row.

Most of the classes in our school were doubled up, one teacher teaching and defending herself from two or three grades at a time, which isn't so difficult when you have children who believe in heaven and hell. Our parents paid for our Christian educations. More often than not we spent our days sitting idly in the church's sanctuary.

Our textbooks were published and shipped in by a fundamentalist college in Pensacola, and scriptures and Bible lessons were worked into every subject, from science to math to history. So in biology class we read the first chapters of Genesis to learn where life had come from, with never a mention that the rest of civilization had come to very different conclusions. And while unsaved children in normal schools learned math through story problems about Mrs. Smith going to market and *how much money will she have left after buying two quarts of milk?* we puzzled over how many fish and loaves of bread Jesus created to feed the multitudes. And history class, of course, was bejeweled with lessons on scripture and morality and the lives of the saints. I remember it was a huge shock to learn in college that George Washington was not really a Southern Baptist and Alexander the Great had never received Jesus as his Savior.

Bill said that it was a mistake, really. His living arrangements. They weren't going to stay with his aunt Shirley. It was temporary. And you smiled at him when he said that.

Aunt Shirley had short hair and she wore pants, and you could tell by looking at her that she was as strong as a man. Thin bones and muscles and a bottle of scotch or gin.

Bill and his mother, Sandy, lived with Aunt Shirley, or rather, they lived around her. Bill tiptoed in their house, walked with a hunch as if to avoid flying shrapnel, while Sandy whirred and whistled between them, negotiating, settling disputes, making peace.

Sandy taught English and Bible and history in our school. She was single, divorced from her husband, but it had been his decision, so she was forgiven. She taught in exchange for Bill's education and was given a stipend of about a hundred dollars a week. Sandy was Shirley's antithesis, petite and feminine and red hair and green feline eyes that laughed and snapped at you. She wore dark brown dresses and clipped her hair short because she was divorced, in mourning, and could not in good conscience remarry. Quiet, a living whisper. The bride of Christ.

"That poor woman," my mother sometimes said. "Without a man."

Mother loved Sandy because she had no man. The two became friends, spent long hours on the phone talking about the difficulties of rearing a son alone, even though neither of them lived alone. Technicalities.

Bill fell in love with my mother, and I fell in love with his. And sometimes we ran out of words around each other, all tied up and gagged and tangled in Freudian jealousy.

I learned English and poetry and writing from Sandy. And more practical things from Bill. We met at the age in which boys are natural eunuchs—sexless, clueless, and safe. Our conversations revolved around comic books and video games, the Incredible Hulk. Sometimes Scooby Doo. Women were just our mothers. Our mothers or those thin-voiced creatures in ankle-length skirts and pink-ribboned pigtails that invaded our classrooms and made better grades than we could manage.

Bill defected in junior high school.

"What do you think of Marsha Parker?" he asked. "Has she got great tits, or what?"

Having never noticed the presence of . . . "tits" . . . on anyone, I said no. Bill frowned, puzzled.

"Well, I think she's got great tits," he said matter-of-factly and gleamed.

Betrayal.

I was lost and wordless in the new conversations. Closed mouth and knotted brow. Bill didn't notice. He was deserting, changing. And he *liked* it.

I hated change. But that didn't seem to matter. Even the boy in my dreams was mutating, growing up, becoming more aggressive, more like a stable version of myself, or of what I wanted to be. And when I was around Bill, a new uneasiness appeared, a guilt that kept pace with the confusion. Needlessly. Bill was always only a friend— always like most other boys, generic tabulae rasae, friends or competitors or enemies. Only occasionally, and unexpectedly, was there a boy who reminded me with his eyes or with his smile that I too was changing. And in those flashes, before the guilt, I also liked it.

For some reason, though, the thought of mentioning Christopher Reeve's great shoulders to Bill did not seem altogether appropriate. So I kept quiet. Listening.

That Christmas Bill's father sent him a copy of *Playboy* in his Christmas stocking. It was nothing short of blasphemy, my mother said, and blasphemy of the highest possible order. To soil the birth of Christ with pictures of women who would certainly not have been candidates for the virgin birth was teetering dangerously close to the unpardonable sin.

"You are not to look at that," she said. "Do you understand me? You are ab-so-lute-ly not to look at that."

And I understood immediately that Bill's magazine was something I would greatly enjoy looking at.

• • •

"What's wrong with you?" he asked.

Jesus, it showed.

"Nothing."

"Check this one out."

There has to be something here. Relax. Keep looking.

"Not your type, huh?" he said and began flipping pages. "OK, you're gonna luuuuuv this one."

Something like a light switch inside your head that is going to click on, just pop right on. Then you're going to see it.

Now just do what he does.

"Wow."

"See? See? What'd I tell you?"

Say what he says.

"Yeah, she's a fox."

And practice this. Practice it at night. Practice their moves and their words and the turn of their heads. Practice it until you feel it, until the light creeps in under the doorway.

I can still do it. I can talk about girls, about women, dissect them with adolescent cruelty. Brag about sexual conquests never achieved and then feel as guilty for the thoughts as for the lies. I can still do it, because I learned it then. I can still act like a man.

three

We rented a truck, a big yellow Ryder truck with a ramp that pulled out from the back bumper. Mom backed it up on the lawn of our house in West Palm Beach, and I pulled that ramp up to the front door.

There was the excitement of an escape, Lisa and I looking nervously over our shoulders to see if Rodney would appear, bringing this dream to a sudden end. We carried out our furniture, our clothes, our beds, finally taking down curtains and curtain rods, rifling through the attic, leaving the house a naked, empty thing, a husk of memories that someone else could live in, never knowing, never guessing, never walking into a closet and sensing or smelling the faint burning echoes of fear.

We moved into a tiny two-bedroom apartment in Tequesta, a town with a dozen or so streets and a church and a little fire station, an exhausted town of young couples and retirees, a town *full* of tiny two-bedroom apartments. And when we stepped inside, when my mother unlocked the door with the shiny new key, the *only copy* of the shiny new key, I could easily have fallen down on the cracked and peeling linoleum floors and kissed each tile individually.

That year. The year that passed too quickly, the year when I cannot recall being afraid, and my mother and Lisa shared one tiny room and I had the other, the year when there was a sense of completion, of karmic credits paid, and peace, and Mother's soft music the only sound through the cardboard walls. The year of fiction? Probably. But it's a fiction that works. And any lesser truth has become the lie.

And I'm going to give these things away. From the wreckage of a childhood, these are all that have truly survived. They are all that I have, and I am giving them away.

I hear the sound of water running hard and fast in the bathroom, where Mom has been secluded for at least two hours. Muffled and breathless, her voice squeaks through the door.

"Do you like your new school?"

"Yeah. I guess. I guess I like it a lot."

"I'm going to be starting school, too."

"What?"

"I said I'm starting school. School. I'm going to school. I'm going to college."

"What? What was that?"

"Nursing. I'm going to be a nurse. I registered today."

She steps outside finally, a towel wrapped around her head, her face pink and clean and gleaming. She is wearing jeans. Blue jeans. My mother is wearing blue jeans. In absolute defiance of everything our church believes, my mother is wearing tight blue jeans with a designer's name on the back pocket and a low-cut purple blouse, and she has long, exotic earrings bouncing against her neck.

"They say there's a real demand for nurses, and this money from the sale of the house isn't going to last forever, so I just thought, what the hell?"

"What did you say? What did you just say?"

And with that, she whips away the towel, letting long wet hair fall around her face, showing off a new chestnut color and tiny, fragile curls that scurry down her back.

"I said, what the hell? Oh, Scott, don't be such a little pharisee. Come on, get the camera. I want to send a photo to my mother."

And I notice for the first time ever that my mother is beautiful— truly beautiful. She is so beautiful when she is not afraid.

• • •

We learn how to sleep. We sleep naturally, without struggle. The men in my mind and in my dreams have softened, less frightening. They are still my private lovers; but now they have grace, now they move with an almost spiritual bearing. Lesser distractions. And maybe God is forgiving.

In the mornings we go our separate ways, we go to classrooms, we three, where we feel welcomed and secure, safe to make friends, proud to make grades that set us apart. We don't flinch anymore at sudden moves, and our eyes are lighter, rested. Mom goes out on dates with men I can admire. They come inside and shake my hand and say, "I'll have her home by ten."

And we laugh at that.

Girls at school think I am handsome, and handsome boys think Lisa is pretty. And sometimes I think this cannot be happening, but then night falls and another morning comes, and still there is nothing ugly to soil the dream.

The women from Mom's college crowd the apartment, drinking wine coolers, smoking the occasional cigarette. Mom is laughing and telling them she has no intention of trying pot. Reality bends over backwards and does a few cartwheels.

Lora, her friend with the heavy makeup, is clucking around me nervously; she pinches my ass and fakes remorse, fakes a Freudian compulsion.

"Look at those eyes." And she is in my face, while Mom's left eyebrow arches like the maternal predator she is supposed to be.

"Look at his eyes. Bedroom eyes. You'd better watch out for this one, Michelle."

And Mom is smiling at me. With unmistakable, unexplainable pride she is smiling at me.

I have made a new friend, Brian. He is strong and blond and takes martial arts classes. He says when he is older he wants to become a marine. Brian shaves his head, and we dream of being marines. The few, the proud. Brian and I work out together after school. I ride the bus home with him sometimes, and we lift weights in a neighbor's gym, then go swimming in his backyard pool.

In the water we wrestle, surrounded by clear blue marble tiles and a masculine, angry affection; two hungry little Spartans up to our necks in Floridian humidity, testing our strength and at least one of us falling in love, mixing forever the sweet excitement of sex with the smell of chlorine.

Then Alba Rodriguez taught me to speak in tongues, and I stepped out into the latter rain.

Alba was the only member of a minority ever to squeak through the admissions process of our private Christian academy. She had light skin, but the school buildings were white and high and rectangular, like rows of giant teeth, and she stood out against them even though she dressed and combed her hair so carefully.

The kids in our school were divided less by our grades than by what we believed. Most of us were Baptists—fundamentalist Baptists, not heretics who belonged to the Southern Baptist Convention. We believed that once you said the sinner's prayer—

> Lord Jesus, I confess that I am a sinner
> I confess that you are Lord
> I ask you to come into my heart and save me

—you were absolutely and eternally saved. No amount of sinning could ever take you out of God's hand. That *would* have made us cocky as hell, except that there was a catch. If you continued to sin, or sinned in a big way, that meant that when you had prayed, you had not been sincere. So we would sin and then say the prayer again, over and over, hoping desperately that one of those times it would catch.

Then there were the Arminians. They were just like Mennonites except that they weren't pacifists, which took most of the fun out of tormenting them. They lived together in Hobe Sound, a huge community built around their church, so we called them "Hobies." Hobies did not believe in eternal salvation; they tended to be nervous people. They didn't believe in sex either, not even after marriage, unless you were trying to have a baby. They had one hell of a lot of babies. They also did not believe in makeup or jewelry, and from birth till death their women were never allowed to cut or trim or braid or perm their hair. So Hobie girls had coils of hair wrapped like cones on top of their heads or hanging down their backs and brushing against their ankles; and they exchanged watches instead of rings at their weddings, which usually came early.

The rest of the kids were almost boring—Presbyterians and Methodists and the occasional Catholic who would wander around the halls, not quite sure why he was there, not quite sure why we were calling him papist. He usually vanished after one or two semesters.

The school would have been ruled by Arminians and Baptists if it weren't for the charismatic kids.

Alba Rodriguez was a charismatic kid, one of many. Charismatic kids went to Pentecostal churches and spoke in tongues, and they were fiercely happy. They congregated in the hallways as if they were novices in some secret society, greeted each other with "Hallelujah's" and "Praise the Lord's" and tithed ten percent of their allowances. They brought books to school, *The Christian's Guide to Positive Thinking* or *Praise You, Jesus for Another Happy Day* or *I'm So Incredibly Happy I Think I'll Just Sit Here and Scream for Jesus*, all written by men who had television ministries and eight-hundred numbers and dubious Ph.D.'s. The Baptist teachers sometimes confiscated them. Pentecostalism was loud and fast, full of miracles and "words from heaven"; it was religion with jet propulsion, God on rocket fuel.

I envied their faith and their warm "Hallelujah's" and dragged Mom and Lisa to their enormous churches, where we sang scriptures set to music and backed up with wailing guitar solos and the crashing and tinkling of drum sets and tambourines.

When they began dancing or wailing or crying out in tongues, we would excuse ourselves and leave.

But Alba Rodriguez was the Terminator of our school's God Squad, and the Holy Ghost told her to follow me.

"You don't know what you're missing until you've received the Holy Spirit," she said. "You've never known the true joy of being a Christian until you've spoken in tongues."

"Not interested," I said. "Sounds obscene."

"It's when the Holy Ghost enters you and speaks through your lips in a language you've never learned."

"Like Spanish or French?"

"No, it's a heavenly language. It's the language of angels. It sounds like babble to other people, but God understands what you're saying because he's making you say it."

"Right."

"Here," she said, "let me show you." Syllables erupted from her smiling lips like machine gun fire.

"And that was God speaking?"

"Yep."

"Any idea what the Most High was saying?"

"Nope. Want me to ask him?"

"No, I think we can stop this before you bring out the turpentine and snakes."

"Laugh all you want. God is not mocked."

"I just can't imagine the Creator of the universe doing something so . . . so incredibly weird."

"That's because you think God is always angry. You don't understand what he's all about."

"And you, of course, *do* understand him."

"Love," she said with a predictable grin. "The God I worship is the God of love."

And I was hooked.

She asked me to meet her in the corner of our high school gym early one morning before classes. She brought another charismatic for backup, just in case the Holy Ghost needed a little prayerful nudging into my Baptist soul.

We clasped hands and they began to pray quietly in tongues, the words falling out all around us, splashing my worldview with a promise of a God who had stopped being angry, a God who would weave a miracle, a sign, proof that he was with me and in me and concerned only with love.

I needed a sign.

Christ, if it's real, fill me. Fill me.

And so the bubble of doubt burst, raining new words, incoherent syllables, flooding my mouth and silencing my brain, slipping across my tongue and out into the air, mixing with the language of Alba and her friend, mixing with the words of angels, mixing together like incense rising slowly from the altar of the oracle at Delphi.

"You have it! You have it!" Alba cried. "You have the Holy Spirit! Do you feel it? Can you feel it?"

And I did feel it. I felt a warm glow coming from deep inside, an almost erotic release. Something was there now, reborn, smoothing out old tensions, forgiving past iniquities, justifying everything. I felt him, God, in me, using me to do his talking, and I felt every ounce of pain groaning in between the words, unutterable, too difficult to speak, but cauterized in the bright light of this new experience.

"I feel it," I said. "God, I can feel everything."

Mom was not convinced, because Satan had a grip on her soul. He tricked her, swallowed up her mustard-seed faith, tangled up her thoughts and called it reason. But she trusted me enough and trusted my new smiles enough to almost be convinced.

She sat once on the corner of her bed with a Bible in her hands and said she would try to receive. We prayed together, and I anointed her with cooking oil, and we read the appropriate passages. Then she opened her mouth wide, looking at me suspiciously out of the corner of her eye, waiting for the words from Jesus to pop in.

"Do you feel it, Mom? Do you feel it?"

We waited and waited, until the sun started to creep down in the sky.

"This," she finally said, "is without question the most ridiculous thing I have ever done in my entire life." And she left me with a mouthful of feathers.

"You've finally cracked," Lisa said with a lift of her hawklike eyebrows that could have frozen the original fire of Pentecost. "I've always known it would happen. It's always been a question of when, not if."

"A prophet," I bit back, "is not without honor, except in his own country."

"Oh, now you're a messiah. Does this mean I get to crucify you anytime soon?"

"You'll repent for that," I said. "Just wait until the last day. You'll see who wins."

"Blow me."

Lisa was damned. So I turned my attention to our classmates instead. Alba and I targeted specific heathens in need of our succor. We wrote their names on three-by-five index cards and held them up toward the ceiling when we prayed.

Bill was the first to go. We trapped him one night in my apartment and read scriptures to him about Pentecost until he caved in and babbled like a believer. He had wanted to talk about his mother and about the rumors about her and Aunt Shirley; but we pushed past all of that, and then he didn't need to talk for himself anymore, not with so much of the Spirit in him.

The other kids at school fell like flies. Baptists, Arminians, Methodists, and Catholics; even frozen Presbyterians—they all went down. I wonder now how many parents I tortured indirectly, forcing them to deal with a fourteen-year-old son or daughter racing home with an unhealthy grin on their rosy cheeks and announcing that they had become the oracles of God. Then, it didn't matter. Then, they were all sinners, they were all in need of something, and for a little while I was the giver, I was the man.

Bill and I coerced my mother into driving us to a new church. It was a monolith, a tabernacle with wine-colored carpeting and red velvet drapes and a parking lot like the one at Disney World. It could seat two thousand, and the thunder-voiced pastor never failed to fill the auditorium. Mom took us Sunday mornings, Sunday nights, Tuesday nights for youth group, Wednesday nights for Bible study, and extraneous nights for good measure.

And the church quickly became the family. The fictitious family, welcome to Mayberry, warm hugs and porcelain smiles and pot-luck dinners and faith healings and other things we were not used to. So we were quiet and claimed our pews, and we learned. And what we learned we believed, because believing was everything we were used to.

I want to paint them colorfully, and I want this to be funny.

I want this to be funny because it has to be funny, doesn't it, all of those grown men and middle-aged women dancing and laughing and swooning and shaking tambourines and talking wistfully about the old-timers, their grandparents in North Carolina or Louisiana. Kentucky. The old ones who had proved their faith with rattlesnakes and turpentine.

"Somebody got a witness! Somebody got a witness!"

And old Mother Brautigan was fat, but when the Spirit come down on her, brother! Can she move!

Or the younger charismatics, Monday through Friday yuppies with college degrees, who smiled kindly at the simpler worshipers and only bounced a little when they danced. Clear-skinned boys, they took themselves so seriously.

They taught us more about speaking in tongues and about the other gifts of the Holy Ghost—the greatest being prophecy, when God would speak through someone in English. Prophets in the church were highly revered, seldom questioned, and unbelievably timely. On a given Sunday morning, the Almighty might mention, via the pastor, that parishioners needed to tithe more, to pay for the pastor's new office, and of course the Holy Ghost would throw in the reminder that all contributions were entirely tax deductible. Or Mrs. Jones might channel a message from the throne concerning the obligation of husbands like, for example, *Mr.* Jones to stop being so irritating to their godly wives. And a teenager armed with the gift of prophecy had little trouble finding dates, since a rejection could always be responded to with "Well, God told me that we're supposed to go out—I suppose you're going to argue with God?"

I need this to be funny.

Hysterical, I mean.

Because it was real and we were there, Bill and I, solid and stoic except when the Ghost came on down. Then we were running, whooping and running to the altar with our hands in the air and the devil off our backs at last. No doubt, no thinking.

We were children.

We were children and we were drenched in love, we were overwhelmed by the gifts on God's platter. So much so that we didn't notice when they slipped us the new set of manacles, the new list of conditions for entrance into heaven. As if we needed any more. They tucked them in our back pockets while we weren't looking.

"You got a call on your life," the pastor says, with his thick hands on my head. "I can see it so clearly."

I hate him now as much as I loved him then. It's two people, really. One of them hates him, because he is here and he will never leave. The other loves him, because he is everything I was supposed to be; the other loves him and loses sleep thinking that maybe—that terrible, terminal, midnight kind of "maybe"—maybe God is on his side, and maybe God is always right, and maybe God's children really are crowded and sweating around the front of the altar right now. In Florida. Dancing.

Hysterical. Really fucking funny.

Pastor set aside a time every Sunday for those whom Satan had afflicted with sickness and disease to walk to the front of the sanctuary, where he would lay holy hands on them and demand from God their healing.

"When you got a promise from God," he bellowed, "when you got a promise from God in the Bible and you can read it in black-and-white, then you can *demand* that he keep his word! You just come on and reach out—*take* your healing. *Take* it. You got the Most High by the short hairs, sisters and brothers. You got the Most High by the short hairs, so you just come on and claim your healing!"

Those who weren't healed waited.

Tent revival was coming. Tent revival, when churches in the scattered counties pooled their resources, set up a tent and covered the ground with straw, and outside there were bales of hay. And they would fly in a professional healer from Dallas or Tulsa; they would fly in a professional.

• • •

"Sickness is the absolute lie." And why give him a name, because he was another Swaggart, another lump of hair spray and polyester. "It is a fraud, a parlor trick of the devil, the enemy's way of taking our eyes off Jesus, the supreme healer."

Bill and I sat near the front to catch every miracle. Bam! There go the holy hands, and there goes another sore back, a sprained ankle— did you see it deflating?—another migraine headache—she's been suffering for years!—more stiffness of the joints, and another leg lengthening.
"Is that Sister Kay, Bill?"
"Yeah, I think so."
"Funny. I've never noticed her limping."
"Well, now she's healed, anyway."
And we clapped our hands, shook our new lambskin tambourines.

From a safe, believers' distance we pitied those who never found relief. Children mostly. They came to the services in wheelchairs, their parents with tight, desperate faces stretched out over bone. Eager and angry, and maybe that was the problem. Not the children, though. Not the ones who could think and speak. They were happy. Twisted and gnarled, some of them, like knots, like roots of trees. But happy and hopeful, and thank you, Jesus.
"Let it go," the pastor said. "Let it happen. God is right here with your healing." He said it with a whine in his throat and a tinge of irritation—as if they were dull, obstinate, slackers.
"Well then, you're just going to have to wait," he would say finally, after they still weren't walking. "Wait, and pray for the Lord to renew your faith."
They waited. Came back the next month, or maybe the next year. The same children and the same parents, and none of them ever did go dancing out the back flap of a door.

• • •

I swallowed inconsistencies, prayed for understanding. When it came, it was broadcast live from Tulsa.

Bill and I found the church where a revival was scheduled. "Look for the satellite dish behind the parking lot," the woman on the phone had said. Inside they had a giant white screen, and they were sucking Brother Shambock in through the airwaves.

"A young couple came to me and said, 'Brother Shambock, why didn't our baby get better? Why did our child die?' " His preacher's voice rumbled through the loudspeakers and the bad wire connection.

"And I told them—your child died because her parents' faith was flaky!" And the audience roared in agreement.

I sat next to Mrs. May, a brown little mouse. Five years before, her daughter had drowned. She told me once that she had dreams sometimes of the policemen standing in a circle beside the lake, slapping her blue baby on the back. In the way you stare straight ahead in a locker room, I did not look in her direction.

"Now, y'all who need more faith come up here, get up close," he said. "Those of you who are joining us by satellite, come up and touch the screen."

We left our pews and moved in close. We prayed in tongues and repented for unbelief. Mrs. May had her hand on a Dolby boom box, and I knew Jesus could forgive her, because she was crying.

In Florida it almost always rains in the afternoon, a cool rain that defies the sunshine, scatters rainbows, and disappears too soon. Some afternoons Bill would walk over to our house, and he and my mother and I would talk and watch the shower, sip Mom's hoarded Diet Pepsis, laugh until everything was funny. Bill had a way of telling a story with a cool irony in his voice, feigned bitterness, a flirtatious and sardonic sense of humor that could crack my mother up in half a heartbeat.

After one of his tirades she started coughing and hacking, and that too seemed funny. We laughed for no reason at her distress, which made her laugh through the coughs, struggling for air until her face was almost blue.

"That's not funny!" she howled, gasping and wheezing. But we were as powerless as if the laughter had come from the Holy Ghost.

Any attempt to stop only made the situation worse, compressed air spurting through our tightly closed lips and starting a whole new avalanche.

"That's not funny! I'm always coughing. I could be sick!"

"Gee, Mom, I'm sorry," I said, becoming very, very serious. "You could be sick. She could be sick, right, Bill?"

"Hmmm, that's right."

"But I wouldn't worry, Mom."

"Well, I guess you're right."

"It's probably just terminal cancer," I said. "You'll be out of your misery in a year."

And at that we laughed, all three of us, we laughed at how sick we all were, we laughed at what a hypochondriac my mother was, we laughed the way people always laugh at evil, some ancient shaman in our bloodstreams telling us it will frighten the demons away. What's the expression? We died laughing.

She said later that week that the young doctor had been nervous, looking down at his clipboard and clearing his throat when he told her that she had terminal cancer and that she would be dead within the year.

f o u r

I went up to the altar of the Lord.

I went up to the altar of the Lord, and there I laid my burden down. I have made supplication before the King of Kings and he is silent, cold as stone, a silver crucifix hollow as hell.

Fifteen years old, and I have already known the frenzy of seeing all that I have, all that I am, and all that I own placed on some divine set of scales, precariously tossed in by the gods to see where they will find a balance.

I walked to our church and the lights were off, but the doors were open. The altar, the platform, had a single light illuminating the gigantic cross that was nailed to the wall above the pool where we submerged the believing, baptizing them into new life.

My knees sank into the cool carpeting of the steps leading up to the podium, and there I prayed with an urgency and a guilty sincerity that I knew could wake the Savior, that I knew could stir even God into action.

The language of angels sweet and living in my mouth, I prayed and fought with the air, I begged and cried and began tracing a line through the past, through every sin, seeking that one unconfessed lie, that one thought or act or gap in action that had led to this warning call of destruction. I let the heavenly language pour out, hoping that in the tangle of consonants and vowels there was something, some unknown word that could unlock this disease and set the captives free. And I prayed for mercy until I believed.

"At least it's unusual," she said. "I'd hate to die of something boring."

"What are these?" Lisa asked her.

"Doctor gave them to me."

She came home with fistfuls of pamphlets with LYMPHOMA written in bold red or black lettering, little two- or three-page booklets that talked invariably about living. Living with the disease.

"Look!" Lisa said. "Your brand isn't supposed to affect women. Never women under thirty-five."

"Lucky me."

"You know where the word 'luck' comes from, don't you?" I said. "From the word 'Lucifer.' "

"That's very nice, sweetheart."

But we had lived long enough with unwelcome strangers, with pain in corporeal form that invaded our lives and invaded my mother. We had lived long enough with some unseen enemy, love or disease or whatever it was called, imbedded in her, sucking her life, killing her inside and killing Lisa, killing me. Hurting inside and hurting irretractably.

"Alright, Mom, I know you don't believe in this, but you've got to listen."

She argued with doctors during the day, and at night we argued theology.

"Disease is caused by a lack of faith. Sin combined with a lack of faith. We've been in sin, we've forgotten God, and this is a warning for us to return before it's too late."

But she didn't see. She thought cancer was caused by mutated cells, and she did not or would not see.

They all wanted her, everyone wanted her blood and her tissues and fragments of her bone. She was rare and she was coveted and she was valuable. She shopped the hospitals as if they were beach resorts, joked that chemotherapy would help her lose weight. The National

Institutes of Health in Maryland finally wooed her successfully. Their facilities were close to Annapolis, and she said they would fly her up twice a week, and the poisons would be free.

She's gone now, she's in Maryland, and the house is mine. She's gone, and Lisa is with her father. I hold my Bible the way you are supposed to, up and away and carefully, like Mary cradling God.

There aren't many listings under *H* in the topical concordance. I only found a few. They don't spend much time dealing with my enemy.

Romans 1:24.

> So God abandoned them to their shameful lusts.
> Men, forsaking the natural use of the woman, burned in their lust one towards another.
> Yes, men committed indecent acts with other men, and received in their bodies their just reward.

Their just reward.
Oh, Jesus. Sweet Jesus. It's supposed to be me.
Something has just gone wrong. I was the one, I was the body that was supposed to have received this punishment, perversion's reward. It should have been me, but you missed. Or the devil missed. Cancer missed—oh Jesus, it should have been me.

Evelyn, my mother's friend, has brought over a tuna casserole and fresh bread. These days everyone is feeding me. I thanked her, but then she started to act sad, she spoke like a mother to me and denied God's power to heal. She left the food on the counter because I hurried her out. I needed her to leave.

Lost, dizzy with praying and reading, I didn't eat until morning. I didn't know that Evelyn's food had soured, the fish and the bread were hard, but everything tasted bitter anyway. And when the vomiting and sweating and shaking began, I thought that it was a demon wrestling with me.

She came home and someone helped her into her room. I stayed in bed waiting for her to come in. When she didn't, I tried to stand but couldn't, the smell from the bucket beside the bed bringing new waves of nausea, new pleas to God, more demands from the Bible, *by his stripes, by his stripes you shall be healed*. No relief. I called out for her and knew she would come as she always had. God did not always answer, but she always came when I called. Then it was night.

The side effects from her chemotherapy wore off after a day, and she was able to walk, with a new fragility, that chemical fragility, down the hall to my room. When she saw me, saw the bucket, the shaking, the signs of dehydration, she stumbled to a phone and called for someone to take me to the doctor.

God will heal me if I have faith, and I have enough faith. You may not have faith, but I do. I have enough faith. I have enough faith for both of us. But I couldn't fight, so they took me anyway. Another defeat.

For years, Honey had been writing us letters, usually addressed to my mother, sometimes to me. They were long, typed out painfully on sheet after sheet of small stationery. She typed with two fingers, sweating and fuming and breaking her nails, and the anger traveled in the ink. They were indictments, usually, listings of sins. Volumes that began with "When you were a little girl . . ."

Lest you forget, Michelle, lest you forget.

And then Bible verses were typed around the corners and edges of the paper or on the backs of the sheets, or even on the envelopes. More than afterthoughts, they were her evidence, her proof that God knew she was right. Exhibits A through Z. They were crooked, because she had to wrestle with the carriage to fit them all in.

In the year without Rodney, Mom had taken to carrying the letters gingerly, snug between her fingertips, from the mailbox to the waste-basket in the kitchen and sending them unread to mulch heaven. The letters thinned and then evaporated; and then there were no more phone calls either.

Until cancer.

"It's your grandmother," Mom said and handed me the phone. Frantic hand gestures accomplished nothing. She forced the phone to my ear and growled.

"You realize this is all happening because of sin."

I tried to be polite, because that is what Christians do. Then my mother took back the phone, sat down with it crooked between her shoulder and ear. She was quiet. Then, "I don't know," she would say, or, "I'm sorry," or, "Well, how do you know I'm not one of the elect?" before she silenced herself again.

She stands in front of the mirror in her bedroom with a pair of scissors.

Her hair is coming out in clumps, soft and plush handfuls of chestnut with brittle velvet at the roots.

"I thought I would keep my hair," she says, looking at her reflection. "They said sometimes you keep your hair."

She snips tenderly where the hair is still full, trying to even everything, trying to make some sense of it, tugging at her bangs, trying to form a frame for her face, but it only comes out when she pulls.

"Let's just get this over with," she says and begins clipping it off, clipping all of it off. "Do you think I could paste it back on?" She wants to make me laugh, but I am dry. "You know, a little Elmer's paste? Who'd know? You wouldn't tell, would you?"

The floor is carpeted with her beautiful mane. Some of it is trapped in her sweater, the rest floats away over her shoulders. She stares then, as if amazed by her ears or by the shape of her head. She smiles, turning her head, shrugging, searching for a way or a pose that still might be pretty; but her face turns cold, and I see a statue, tragic and abandoned. A picture-perfect statue—white, chemically robbed skin and lashless eyes.

"Maybe she's right," she says. "Maybe this is sin."

She announced a few weeks later that we would be moving to Maryland.

The flights, she said, the flights up and down the coast had become too exhausting. She was weaker with every treatment, the flight attendants ushered her gently to the back row, where she would fill bag after bag with vomit that smelled like antiseptic and acid. She said her prayers and recited the names of the chemicals like a litany against fear, against encroaching death; she recited them and hung to them, mustard-seed gas and methotrexate.

My grandfather came to get us in a white van that could only hold a few things. The rest we gave away or sold, piece after piece of our created world vanishing through the front door while some friend or stranger smiled and said thank you and left feeling they had really helped us out. I hated them. They were carrying my life under their arms, parts of her and parts of me, given a price tag and stolen, I thought, by those who had no faith. I hated the doctors, the hospital that was a huge white tabernacle built in honor of faithlessness, I hated the medicines that promised to heal while they only hurt, and above all I hated my grandmother with her insults and acid condemnations.

So I sat in the van with my grandfather grinding my teeth, while Lisa and Mom followed in our car. I-95 changed with the miles and the state signs, the scenery becoming different, full of hills and forests, autumn leaves—colors unfamiliar and depressing. The highway, I thought, was lined with a thick wall of dying things. In the Carolinas we turned on the heater, and hot wind blew into my eyes and ears, signaled the approach of Hades. Rational thought was left far behind, in the Sunshine State—everything was seen in high contrast, everything was black or white, faith or doubt, heaven or hell, with nothing in between.

"Let's get some things straight," Honey said when we arrived at last. We gathered around the dining room table, pulled our chairs up close to the antique edges.

"We're going to set some ground rules," she announced. "Michelle, you've got to get your life right with God. He may heal you yet, but don't count on it. You've never truly repented for your sins; you've just heaped one on top of the other, and now God's taken drastic measures to get your attention."

"God doesn't make people sick," I said. "The devil does."

"And worst of all," Honey continued, looking only at my mother, "worst of all you've let your son be carried off with a doctrine of Satan. He's been warped by charismatic heresy."

I looked to my mother for help, but she was only nodding and staring down at the table. She was cold, her pink woven cap a poor replacement for her natural covering. Her teeth clicked against each other, and she was tired. And she was somewhere else anyway, she was in 1968, listening to her mother, doing as she was told. Going, going, gone.

"In this house," Honey said, turning her attention to me, "you will not practice your demonology. You will study God's word under qualified teachers, and you will learn the truth."

"Just a shame," my grandfather said, head shaking. "Just a crying shame."

"Oh, I wouldn't worry." And now she looked at him as if she were a doctor, a surgeon. "You'll see. Just wait and see."

My room was in the basement, and the ceiling was wood and pipes and electrical wires. The floor was black marble, an afterthought from the time when the house had been beautiful, Victorian and grand, instead of ancient and frozen in dust.

It was December, and the floor was cold enough to hurt when you walked on it, cold enough to stick to your feet if you lingered more than a second. And that was perfect. Because pain was what was needed. Pain was what the doctor ordered. Pain would prove to God my conviction. I knelt on the floor and spoke to the sky, prayed as if Maryland were a suburb of Gethsemane, prayed until I thought I could feel blood congealing on my forehead or in the palms of my hands and there were raw red welts on my knees.

Welcome to the Inquisition.

Lisa and I commuted to a fundamentalist school—"a good, solid school"—that was hours away by bus. The school building was made of aluminum. Thin garage walls made of tin and a concrete floor; they had set it up behind a church.

The church was Baptist, all of our teachers were Baptists, and the uncertain salvation that dried up their faces was Baptist. There were severe penalties for falling asleep in the classroom, written out in bold lettering in their plastic-bound handbooks, ruthlessly enforced because the metal walls couldn't keep out the Maryland winter, so they kept the heat running high until you struggled and smothered under it and the air had sponged up all the moisture from your eyes. And some anonymous someone had warned our Bible teacher that I had once been a Baptist.

So he gave us lessons from the book of Acts, the book used by charismatics to justify miracles, speaking in tongues, and divine healings. He was a thin man. And while making his best points, after clearing his throat and gripping his podium and trying to raise his papier mâché voice to draw his most obvious conclusions, he would walk close to my desk and stare big black holes into me.

"There are *others* who believe . . ." And you could fill in the blank with whatever I believed.

"But *we* know . . ." And in went the talons, while the Christian children snickered. They knew I was an "other" and could never be a "we."

It was a quiet school with a quiet-colored dress code, and it was quietest of all to those of us who by complexion or status or religion could never be numbered among the "we."

I smuggled books by Oral Roberts and Jimmy Swaggart in my gym bag, hid them under my shirt and read them in the stalls of the boys' room. At home they were hidden in secret pockets of my suitcase, and Mom kept some of them for me in her room, in her makeup case.

And there was a boy, Erik. He wore a coat like a parka with a big fur hood. Erik the Viking, Erik the Great. He always sat in front of me. Black hair and blue eyes, and ivory muscles in his neck. And I hated myself for loving the curve of his neck.

The dinner table was the judgment seat. You're damned, all of you, now pass the peas.

When Mother was weak, Honey waited by her bedside, read her

favorite verses, held her hand while she vomited, and put cool wash-cloths on her forehead.

When she was stronger, when she could come to the table, Honey ripped at her with scriptures, disemboweled her over steak and scalloped potatoes.

Honey lived with her Bible, in her room, on her bed. With a big black Bible and a big black tape recorder and a little black notebook with tight blue lines on the pages.

Those were the sounds of those days. I remember them from holidays and weekends: the frantic turning of pages, the tapes of methodical Calvinist preaching, the scribbling of her pen. And the occasional fevered whisper, "Yes! Yes, that's it!"

She brought her notebook to the table, and that was the discussion for the evening.

"Here's why I know beyond any shadow of a doubt that you are wrong." And then more sounds of pen against paper while I looked down at my plate, because she made black marks next to her reasons as she read down the page.

And you do not speak. You do not speak until ready to say, "Yes, of course, you're right, how foolish I've been."

You never speak.

Now faith is the essence of things hoped for. The evidence of things not seen as yet . . .

You don't know what faith is.

Faith is my hope.

Faith is my stiff-lipped denial.

Faith is salvation.

And salvation is praying the breath into her body one more morning, one more evening, one more day. Just one more day.

And, Christ—with all of the sickness that hung in the air of that house like black cigar smoke, why were they so concerned, so obsessed and desperate, with taking *my* medicine away?

Because faith is the evidence of no other options, hard-core opiate for serious addicts. I was a heretic, tripping on acid. *Good* Christians want heroin, tinfoil, and tears.

. . .

Mother was late coming to the table. And the door was closed in my grandfather's study. When she came out, she stood in the doorway and supported herself on her cane.

"There's someone on the phone for you, Scott," she said.

"Who is it?"

"It's your father."

Now here's a voice that fits.

"Hi," he said. And then there was silence.

Still, it fit. Here, for a change, is a memory that doesn't eat you like cancer; it just ripples up and rings in your ears. As if acceptance of his tones and accents was something inborn, genetic.

"I haven't talked to you in a while," he said. "How . . . uh, how are you?"

You mean, who are you? It's alright. You can say it.

"I'm fine."

"I'm getting married," he said.

"I thought you were already married."

"Lynn and I are getting a divorce. She has custody of our two sons. I'm engaged. To a marine."

"Really? A marine? What's she like?"

"Well, she's a power lifter. Weighs about two ten. The facial hair takes some getting used to, but all her tattoos match, so I can't complain."

"OK," I say, then forget to speak.

"That was a joke, Scott."

Requisite laughter. Help me. I don't know who you are, but I want you to help me.

"I'd like you to meet her. Your mother says you can come and spend a weekend with us. We only live a couple of hours away."

"That'd be great."

"Good. How about next weekend?"

"Great."

"OK, we'll see you then."

"Alright. Good-bye. Dad . . . I love you." And I don't know where those words came from.

"I . . . love you too," he said, after a pause; but then it was the voice of someone who has been taken off guard. It was the voice that said, underneath the nervous chuckle, no. No, that was too easy.

We prepared for my father's arrival like nervous Christians preparing for the second coming. I pestered my mother with questions, looking for clues, his likes and dislikes, predictions of his expectations, making an outline for the present from her memory of a teenaged lover. At night in my room, I sat up late in the dark, practicing answers and questions.

"Oh, of course I make straight A's. It's a Peck tradition, isn't it?"

"No, I've never been in any kind of trouble. My life's been just great."

"Girls? Yeah, girls. Gotta love 'em, eh, Dad? Sure, sure. Lots and lots of girlfriends. One after the other. Girls, girls, girls."

Other men dreamed about having the kind of paragon of a son—perfect and respectful and dutiful and painfully heterosexual—that I was going to deliver, wrapped and packaged like a Christmas present, to my father the marine.

That week, Gamp drove my mother to Bethesda to get a wig. NIH had a program for female chemo patients called Magical Me or something equally happy, and she sat in front of one of their mirrors for a long, long time. Her father finally said he liked the long blondish one with loose waves, and curls around the front that hung down to her eyebrows. So she asked for that one, and the nurses cooed around her and said she was pretty.

She put it on on Friday afternoon while I sat in her room pretending to pack the suitcase that I had already prepared three days before. She used tweezers to pluck carefully around her cheeks and above her lip.

"Incredible," she said. "The steroids give me hair everywhere except on top of my head."

"Do you think he'll be early?"

"No, your father's always on time. And why couldn't I get the kind of cancer that makes you *lose* weight?"

"You look fine."

"I wonder. Did he tell you what she looks like?"

"No, not really."

"A huge chest, I'll bet."

"What?"

"Nothing. Well, what do you think?" She turned around in her chair and smiled. "Well, wait, I'm not nearly done yet."

"Do you think he'll like me?" I asked.

She turned around again.

"Of course," she said as if she had forgotten that I didn't know him. "He's always loved you, really. Really. He's just not . . . good at that kind of thing."

It took her a long time to come downstairs. I helped her with each step, one, two, three, and then she would have to stop and sit down and breathe. They were old, winding stairs, Victorian stairs. Gamp sat with Honey in the kitchen and made his strong coffee.

We sat in the living room and waited, looking around at nothing. Honey was reading the scriptures, silent. That made us nervous, because there is danger in her silence.

Finally the doorbell rang.

"I can't believe it," I heard Honey in the kitchen. She stood up suddenly and walked around quickly in two or three tight circles, wringing her hands. "I can't believe he's going to be inside my house."

Gamp tried to calm her, but she pushed at him, "I can't believe it," and then thumped quickly up the spiral staircase in her pink bedroom slippers.

The doorbell rang again, but I waited. My mother was frozen. Gamp started up the stairs, and I reached for the door handle, but then he walked back toward my mother.

"Michelle," he hissed, leaning over her, smiling. "Michelle, you look like a circus clown."

Somewhere inside here there must be a more perfect picture of the day you came.

I remember the cold air that pushed me back when I opened the heavy oak door. I remember your wife, Joanne, with her pixie smile and close-cropped black hair, peering around your shoulder. She had a wide stance, a power stance, a man's stance, I thought, as she rocked boyishly from one foot to the next against the cold. A man's stance, and such a pretty woman's smile.

I remember the smell of my grandparents' living room, the smell of mothballs, thick, an oppressive air for an oppressive place. But I've already said all of that.

I remember that Lisa wanted to meet you. And that that was the day I realized she had a picture-perfect hero's image of you too; she had eavesdropped on my mother's stories. She wanted to see you, but she was not allowed. She read her Young Girl's Bible and stayed in her room.

And I remember fury still hot on my face. My grandfather's words to my mother stuck, stiff needles in my mind. Maybe it passed for the pink that comes with cold mornings, but there was something there that must have looked and smelled a little like murder, a strong desire to leave you, leave this, find my grandfather, ferret him out, make him pay for crushing my mother's painted and practiced dignity so indifferently, seconds before her childhood walked in the door.

I can remember my mother regaining her face, picking it up with the muscles in her temples and trying to look like herself, like a Magical Me, trying to look just like herself, something like the memory.

But I can't remember you.

I can't remember you except to say I remember the forgotten handshake and reaching out, wrapping both arms around you, reaching and wrapping both arms around you in an embarrassing embrace. Too close, too soon, too desperate for salvation.

I was irritated when my mother asked me to play the piano for you. I am good. I am too good. Suspiciously good. The piano is all wrong. So I show you a football trophy, now two years old, I think, but there it is, a testament to testosterone, and see? I have become a man.

And now I remember.

He is effortlessly a man. Natural and male and transparent. With a restrained and dignified smile and a carpenter's handshake and hair shaved clean along the sides.

The three adults are nervous. They shift in their seats and clear their throats, and his new wife or wife-to-be is pleasant and friendly with the old wife. And the old wife too is pleasant and she is friendly, and I wonder if they hate each other, but they do not.

They talk but I hear nothing. I smile and look at his face. My mother laughs shyly and jokes, and then my father is more nervous and looks younger, seventeen or eighteen, then looks embarrassed or surprised at himself and straightens up in his seat and holds his new wife's little hand and looks distant, or looks like a marine.

And some awkward vision crumbles as soon as I recognize it; these two would see each other and know each other and fall in love together and we would all leave. And the new wife would not exist because that is not what was meant to be. The new wife would go in peace, and everything would come back together the way it was meant to be. The way God wanted it to be. Only because it was the will of God, not because of what I wanted, not because of me.

In my father's house there are lacquered signs, wood, with the Marine Corps emblem etched and painted in gold and red around a circle and an eagle unfolding itself in the center with straight-lined, featherless wings.

On his ashtrays and glassware there is the same design. And stacks, in the kitchen, of official-looking papers and *Leatherneck* magazines piled up on one another in order, by month: October, November, now Christmas, December. Black polish for boots in the closet and suits starched flat under invisible plastic; solid crowded rows of khaki green.

"Just make yourself at home," Joanne says; so I try, sit down on their sofa, far to the right, near a corner, and cross and then uncross my legs while they make closing-cupboard, squeaking-oven-door noises in the kitchen.

Soft voices in the kitchen.

It is a home you might see on TV. A home for some sitcom family or a weekly drama—that structured, that clean. I have seen houses like this in magazines. *So*, I think, *this is how other people live;* and then quickly repent, *Lord Jesus forgive me, Lord Jesus forgive*, because there is betrayal in that stray-cat thought. And envy. But, still . . .

I would love to live in this house. I would love to live in a house like this, like a picture in a magazine. And I would come down the steps in a football jersey, or soccer or rugby, with Marine Corps muscles and shorter hair and keys to a car. And I would smile and say something perfect to my father and mother as I went out the door.

"I thought you played beautifully," she says, this woman who is not my mother.

"Thanks."

"Have you ever played the organ?"

"No."

"Come on. I'll show you. It's not so different."

Carefully—*carefully*—she invited me to sit next to her on the organ bench that was only big enough for one. It creaked and complained under our weight.

"Do you read music?" she asks.

"No. I learned to play in church. By listening."

And then she turned it on, the relic of a machine whistling and humming, lazily, sputtering, like an old man.

This is wrong. He will hear. He will see.

But she tapped her feet on black pedals, testing, pulled out knobs and levers to adjust the sound.

"It's really easy." And her voice is sweet.

This is wrong. Who are you to me?

"You try the harmony."

On the upper board, she stretched out her fingers. And in time I put my hand on the lower keys, adding new awkward sounds and bass and entirely fictional harmonies.

And when we had finished, and my father, who had been quiet, said dinner was ready, she talked about music while she laid out the table. Everything, even the throwing down of placemats, a comforting, well-practiced routine.

But the conversation was not well practiced. It was difficult and stiff and disorderly.

"So, Scott," Joanne finally said. "How do you like school?"

"Just fine."

Silence.

"Are you doing well?"

"Usually."

"That doesn't surprise your father—does it, Fred? You told me Scott was very intelligent, didn't you?"

"Uh-huh."

"Your father did very well in school, you know."

"I've heard."

"So Fred, what *was* it like for you at the academy?"

And he began, speaking through her to me. And I answered through the same channel.

And if that now seems like a dream, and my writer's imagination questions its reality, then I can instantly seek out the truth. It is where she laid out a place for me, with words too soft to be spoken. Too fragile and volatile, too sacred now in memory; sounds, and the warm birthplace of a friendship, hiding like angels in between the black-and-white keys.

I woke up early, because that is what you are supposed to do when you are the perfect son of a perfect marine. He was up already, standing in his red-and-gold bathrobe in the kitchen with his coffee. He smoked a cigarette, a Marlboro, but that similarity with Rodney was instantly forgiven. I was up early but didn't know what you are supposed to do when you are up early. So I leaned against their cupboard, counted tiles on the floor.

"It's hard to talk," he said, when it was far too late to say good morning. "A lot of bridges burned."

"Bridges can be rebuilt," I said, and that was something like the truth. But it was still too close, too fast, too easy—you have to earn that kind of truth.

Back in Maryland, judgment crouched, waiting.

Mother's silence swelled; sank further after every weekend with the marines. Dark thoughts, heavy thinking.

• • •

The principal came to our class and motioned for me to come out into the hall to meet him.

"Collect your things," he said. He was a nervous little man, who never looked the children in the eye.

"Did I do something wrong?"

"No, no, nothing like that. The doctors said you should go to the hospital. To see your mother."

"Oh."

"Let's pause right here and say a little prayer, alright?"

I looked around when he closed his eyes. Saw Honey's Cadillac parked outside.

"They've given her a handful of days," she said in the car. My grandfather plowed the tank through the narrow streets to Bethesda.

"Her days are in the hands of God," I quoted. "The doctors don't know more than God."

Honey blew out disgust through her lips in a tight hiss.

"Your mother," she said, "has lived a life of sin. And if it takes this to keep her from continuing in sin, then I hope God *does* take her home. Even if it breaks my heart."

What heart? I thought, a commoner's thought. *Hush, child.* I was still too young to drive.

Pneumocystis pneumonia. That was the first time I heard those words. In a thicket of other words more potent, and mixed together with hourly reports to those of us waiting in the ICU lobby, something about blood gases and predictions of life. Lymphoma eats at an immune system like a snake, inches its way along the lymphatic alleyways, crude stomach bulging, refusing retreat once its jaw has opened and locked. Pneumocystis pneumonia. They thought that was what was killing her.

The doctor never told us to go home. He suggested we wait. He was a young man with an athlete's build and a childlike complexion. In someone else's life, he would have been handsome. Too young to be a doctor, too young to be so experienced with death. Still, young enough that life's comings and goings were not just another day's business, a worn-out clinical routine.

So he patted me on the shoulder on his way out of the lobby, patted me once and squeezed; and I thought it was criminal, the resignation in his face. Sad and natural, and no faith—or some different kind of faith. In memory I love that face. I love acceptance, learned and etched on that clear-water face.

We went in to see her in shifts, according to the rules. I held her hand and *believed* her there, believed her to be there, watching from inside her coma like a bear in a cave; watching over the mask and the tubes and the dry white of her cheekbones.

"You're not leaving," I whispered in between unintelligible prayers. Still, she looked like chalk. Stubbornly, she would not move. "You're not going anywhere."

In an empty room next to the nurse's station, with a vacant bed and the lights shut off, I found a phone and called my father.

"I've been there," he said, uncertainly. "My mother died of cancer last year."

She's not dying.

"It's awkward. But I'd like you to think about where you're going to live after she's gone."

Vulture.

"Joanne and I would like you to come and live with us."

He's a vulture. And I'm no better.

"I'd like that," I said. "I think I'd really like that."

When they took away her respirator she continued to breathe; fluttered and fought to open her eyes. She would not believe she had been dead for a week.

"Did you see anything?" I asked, hoping for a vision.

"I can't even remember going to sleep."

"I was here," I said. "I was here, I was praying. Could you hear me?"

"I'm sure I did." And she smiled around the throat tube until she looked like herself again.

"You're a traitor!" she screamed, until the coughing began and took her wind again. Then she was red faced and glaring and clutching at the metal rail rim of her bed. "Are you trying to kill me?"

The day began in peace with breakfast with my father and Joanne after a weekend where we had been trapped inside because of the rain. We played Trivial Pursuit, and my father took jabs at my Christian school education while Joanne frowned and pretended she didn't mind losing to him.

Then we drove to the hospital and walked through the white labyrinth at the National Institutes of Health until we found my mother's private room. Outside in the hallway Honey and Gamp accosted us, pulled my father away.

"We'd like to speak to you, Fred."

"Alright."

I slouched against a white brick wall.

"What are you going to do about him?" Honey asked, pointing at me. "What are you going to do about him and his godless, disrespectful—"

"Disrespectful? Jesus Christ, he's afraid of his own shadow. He seems like a good kid. Despite his environment."

"He's got the wool pulled over your eyes, then."

"Funny. This feels a lot like history repeating itself," my father said, and solidified history.

So it happened. It all really happened.

"Tell you what," he said. "I'll just take this burden off your hands. In two weeks, he comes to live with me."

And I followed him when he turned on his heel and walked away.

He was smiling.

He went into my mother's room and came out again a few minutes, too few minutes, later, his eyebrows raised half in embarrassment, half in relief.

"I think you should start packing."

He shook my hand and left, and I stepped cautiously into her room.

"Traitor!"

"What?"

"Just leave. Just get away from me."

When she came home from the hospital she was sequestered again in her room under a mountain of pillows and warm blankets and Christian books. The books went unread, and she kicked off her blankets, silent and smoldering, indifferent to her mother's rebukes.

The principal of our school called me into his office the next day.

"Your grandparents have told me your history," he said through his nose. I stared at him, staring him down, watching his absurd cowlick dance back and forth while he spoke. "You can't possibly believe your father cares anything about you. You don't abandon your son and then show up thirteen years later pretending to be father of the year."

"My grandparents say a lot of things."

"What are you implying?" And then he puffed up like a pigeon, snorts and coos and righteous indignation. "That's a very serious insinuation you're making, son."

He leaned forward, hands folded on his desk. Almost met my eyes.

"I'd be careful," he said. "I'd be careful if I were you."

"I'm sorry," I said. But inside I know. I know that you don't know my history. I know that my grandparents make donations, and they make them big because they can buy anything with their money. I know they pay your bills, you bastard.

You Baptist.

We sat together in silence, as I sat with my father in silence, but this was strange for us, alien. This was not our ritual, it was not our way.

"I can't believe you're leaving me," she said, and the sweetness in her voice crumpled all defense. "I know I'm being selfish, but I can't believe that you would leave me."

"I don't want to," I whispered. "I just can't take it here."

There was a small light in her room. Weak yellow-orange on alabaster walls.

"When I get better, we can go home."

"They don't want you to get better."

"I don't know. I don't think that. I don't know."

"I can't stay here. I'll go crazy. I've got to leave."

We sat a little while longer, and the conversation drifted back and forth, away and further away from the subject of my defection. And then, outside of any context, she asked for my hands.

She pulled, with pain, and swung her feet out toward the floor. Her body was full of fluid, water heavy. More pain when she bent her knees, and sharp, shocked inhales before her feet could touch the floor.

And then we said nothing.

I sneaked into her room afternoons during Honey's radio Bible hour. Held her hands, let her lean on me until she could stand, then stumble, then walk. After a week, she tried the stairs. We stood together at the ledge and stared down the winding steps.

It took almost an hour. And she cried, avoiding my eyes for shame. Avoiding my eyes, so needlessly, for shame.

It had rained the day before, a freezing rain that left the ground a solid block of ice with houses and trees and asphalt jutting obscenely skyward or scarring the ground that was otherwise a perfect mirror. In the morning it snowed and laid a cotton robe over the bare back of the ice, a slick divine deception.

I salted and hacked away at the back steps until they were safe, and suggested we try this some other day.

"You're crazy," my grandmother told her, when she saw her walking. "Stupid and irresponsible and crazy."

And then my mother had to try.

"Give me my keys."

We negotiated the steps and began the cautious walk to the car. Her arm locked around my neck, she paused and lifted a shaking foot over every tiny embankment, every dry-stick obstacle. The ice pulled her away, yanked and dragged her in different directions. Under the snow, her Ford LTD was still there, frozen like time, frozen like a coma, like dependency. The keyhole to the door was iced, solid and impenetrable.

"Go heat the key."

I left her leaning on the car and ran inside to run the key under hot water and grab the blue tumbler of Morton salt. When I came back, huffing and breathless, she was gone. I ran around the car and found her lying on her back in the snow, visible clouds of air puffing rapidly skyward.

"Mom!"

She was laughing.

"This is a new low," she howled. "This is definitely a new low for me."

I tried to get her up, but her muscles were busy shaking. She started coughing, clutched at my arm, pulled, then gave up and flopped back down, now positively hysterical.

"My mother better not come out here and try to stop me," she suddenly whispered. "I'll kick her ass!" And then we were both goners, sides and ribs aching, loving it, sitting stupidly in the snow and laughing while we watched the Morton's break the lock.

She drove around the block again and again. Filled the tank and kept driving.

"This feels wonderful," she said, tapping her fingers on the steering wheel. "This is a lot easier than walking."

We stopped at a Hardee's and ate everything on the menu her doctors had told her was forbidden, bags of french fries and chicken legs and a huge frosty milk shake that made no more sense than anything else we were doing. When we came back home she limped less painfully past her mother's scowls, up the spiraling staircase to her room.

"You can call your father," she said, cocooned again in bed. "You can tell him you won't be coming."

"What do you mean?"

"I mean I'm getting out of here. We're getting out of here. We're going home."

And I was happy, before the shame. Cold shame. Because after she had woken up, I never had even the slightest intention of leaving.

"God has only spared your life because you've been here with us," Honey said over and over like a mantra; and when the appointed day drew close, she said it desperately. "If you go back to Florida, and back to your sinning, you'll die. I promise you that."

My father was skeptical about our move, but he never put up a fight. We just shook hands and said good-bye casually, with promises to keep calling and writing and visiting.

"It's a short plane ride," Joanne said. "It's not so far from West Palm Beach."

The day we left, she called the hospital. I didn't know she had planned to quit her chemotherapy but thought it was a grand idea, a true sign of faith.

"Their healing is killing me," she said, and I knew she was speaking truths from the Spirit. It wasn't just the side effects of chemotherapy that made her so sick, so close to death. It was the lack of faith that inspired them, pumping disbelief three times a week into her veins.

We packed what we could carry, Lisa and I each grabbing things that were the most precious to us. Books mostly. The rest of the furniture our grandparents agreed to keep in storage in their basement until our certain return.

"Your mother will see," Honey said. "She'll come back when she realizes she's sinning, and we'll take her back, if it's not too late."

We left in the middle of the afternoon, because Mother had become nocturnal in her convalescence and because she wanted quick driving on deserted roads. I carried out our luggage, helped her to the car, merrily oblivious to everything—my selfishness, our absurdity, our desperation—everything but her suffering. And that, that cancer, that small thing, I knew would dissolve, once away from this snow and this hate and this angry gray-haired preacher of the *God* of hate. All of it, even cancer, would dissipate in Floridian sunshine.

We pulled out of the long driveway, and I did not look to the windows, I do not remember any good-byes.

Half a mile down the road, Mother realized she had left her purse and her money on the kitchen counter. We drove back, and I was sent inside to retrieve them.

I entered the back door without knocking and tiptoed through the kitchen, hoping to avoid any final confrontations. Just when I thought my escape was clear, Honey appeared around the corner, and I jumped as if surprised by a burglar or a demon.

"What are you doing?"

"My mother left something that belongs to her."

"Take it. Go."

And now, looking back, I have lived just enough of a life to put her spirit in context, to make excuses and allowances. Just barely enough to see the usefulness, the *necessity*, of compassion. I see her cold stare and warm it beside my own private fires.

But that is now. Then, I was a child, with a child's eyes and a child's understanding and a child's snow tracks on her linoleum kitchen floor. So I acted like her grandson, reflected her anger, and her grief suppressed and cloaked as anger. And fear—which in her has always been less a weapon, more a disease that is tragically contagious. And I ran.

I ran away from all of that, and ran to escape, and ran to my mother's car, where the heater was already running and Lisa was peering over the backseat waiting, and as we pulled out on our long, long journey, it never occurred to me to ask her where we were going.

I must have assumed we were going to heaven.

We arrived at Rodney's new house on schedule.

He was waiting with the key to let us in, and I grumbled some sort of thanks. He said he was living with his girlfriend now, so he couldn't stay there with us. Mother's face tightened up at that. So he promised. From time to time he would try to stop in. And then she smiled and thanked him.

Lisa and I commuted to our old Christian school, and old friends and teachers oozed sympathy, put their arms around our necks, and welcomed us back in. Concern and caring and promises of prayers, and "So what did you think of snow?"

Dead. White and dead.

But Florida was better than medicine, my mother's body filling out into a woman's shape again, the sun waking up the pigments in her skin. Her hair grew back slowly with a new color, salt-and-pepper. The sign of winter, she said.

She washed her old blue jeans and polished her heels. Looked up an old boyfriend. A small, rough man, who had said he loved her, before the disease. He came to pick her up one night to take her to the state fair, and I disapproved, since her divorce was not final. But she looked so much like herself that night that I stifled the Holy Ghost, went into my room, and asked God to understand.

She came home late with a huge stuffed animal crammed under her arm, the kind the fair occasionally lets someone win to keep everyone playing games. Charlie, her date, disappeared, and she sat and talked with us in the living room, while I frowned like a Christian.

We didn't notice that Rodney was inside the house until it was too late, and he was blocking the door.

"Who the fuck was that?" And the voice of judgment filled up the air, froze us into place like rabbits in front of headlights.

"I said, who the fuck was he? I just saw him leaving!" He grabbed my mother, and she went limp. He pulled her up, dragged her like a doll into the kitchen. Lisa was already outside. But then Lisa was always smarter than we were.

"What do you care?" I heard her screaming, repeating.

"You're fucking cheating on me!"

"You're living with your girlfriend and you say I'm cheating on you?"

"You're not going to whore yourself out from my house, Michelle."

"Did you just say 'whore'?"

I saw her grab him by his lumberjack shirt, pull him toward her face.

"You've got no right," she said. "You've got no rights. You gave them all away."

"I—"

"If you ever touch me or my children again, I'll kill you."

And she walked past him, through the living room, to the door.

"I'm dying, you limp-dicked son of a bitch," she called back over her shoulder and smiled. "Don't try me. I've got nothing to lose."

"Not in my house, woman!" he bellowed, but it was empty, it was too late. He caught me by the arm as I tried to make my own escape.

"Do you see my point?" He was shaken, confused. His breathing was all alcohol fumes and pants. "Do you see my point?"

"Whatever you say."

"I say I'm right."

"Then you're right," I said, because I was afraid for my life. "Then you're right. Whatever you say."

I caught up with my mother, who was walking with Lisa to a pay phone.

"I'm sorry," I said. "I told him he was right."

She said it didn't matter. Then she called the police, and two men in blue uniforms escorted her into the house to collect our things.

• • •

We moved in with Charlie that night, and that lasted a few weeks. Then we moved in with a church family, I can't remember their names. Doesn't matter. The next week we lived with someone else. I called my father on weekends, making new and creative excuses why we didn't have a phone number, why he couldn't call, hoping he wouldn't guess that we were living like vagabonds, living out of our car, living off people's charity.

"He shouldn't be there," he said to my mother. "He shouldn't be around you right now."

"Don't take him away, Corky."

"You can't take care of yourself."

Mom found a job in a gas station that week as an all-night cashier. And she said she had repented, put her eyes back on Jesus.

She sat behind the counter with her *Living Bible* and "witnessed" to the customers who came in to buy cigarettes or beer.

"I'm dying," she would say to them. "But I know I'm going to heaven. If you died tonight, do you know where *you* would go?"

And sometimes they put back their beer.

We made new friends and went to new churches, depending on whom we were living with. I would walk in behind her, holding her portable oxygen tank, and the brothers and sisters approached her shyly, introduced themselves. She had a smile that I remember, with its own center of gravity.

Pastors started coming to see her wherever we were staying, and parishioners brought us food and clothes and money.

"That brave woman. That brave sweet woman," they whispered outside the door.

She spoke in churches, of every denomination. A Baptist for Baptists, a glowing firefly for Pentecostals. And when she spoke it was with simplicity and beauty and an absence of fear. A local Christian radio station interviewed her on the air, giving a devotional, and then we were deluged with checks and letters and fan mail.

"I'm so happy," she said, although she always blushed at their applause. "This is just like when I was dancing."

She practiced her sermons at home, strong and clear through her oxygen mask. Strength in a child's voice—parables that could melt you and feed you and then cut you unexpectedly at the next turn. Could cut through the terror of living, the stagnant boredom of the day-to-day. Brought heaven's intrusion to the day-to-day.

"I'm just a woman," she said. "Still just made of clay."

Clay. A broken vessel, illuminated—illuminated by Death, who was near and stalking. Under his dark breath, raptured and made preternatural like one of Nero's burning Christians.

But I couldn't see it then.

She was dying day by day. I didn't see it, I could not or would not; blanked it all out, even when her breathing became more labored and a new doctor said her tumor was growing, her immune system fading. Even when we moved into the house of another set of friends, wealthy Christians who set up a hospital bed and an oxygen tank in the middle of their living room. Even when her days were taken up with people visiting and seeking her prayers, her prayers for healing, seeking to tell her their lives and their pain and their suffering and confessions like notes to take with her to heaven—even then and for all of that, it never occurred to me that she was dying.

five

The last few weeks and days and minutes are cartoon memories, the kind you see when you go window-shopping through your childhood, the scenes colorful and safe and full of the sounds of angel's wings brushing against each other as they fuss and huddle around you.

I have seen paintings on velvet of angels guiding children across a bridge that teeters over raging water, standing between them and the broken railing, poised to protect, Christ's eyes painted in the clouds—watching out, we know, for all the tender hearts, for every footfall of every sparrow, leaning over earth to catch every widow's prayer, every orphan's cry.

It is never really like that. Not until you have crossed the bridges and grown up and fallen in and out of love and spent nights studying tiny cracks in the ceiling by yourself in a room that you used to share with another warm body—seen other children and other sparrows fall through the cracks of God's fingers and suffer. Then you look at yourself and into yourself, then you go walking through your past and think you see angels, because you've been lucky.

But there were no thoughts like these, not then. Not when I walked home, or to the home where we had temporarily set up camp, and confronted the reality of her plummeting condition, the oxygen mask and the IVs and the huge metal-frame bed that filled up this stranger's living room. It was a simple choice then between falling apart or tightening all the fantasies, all the strings.

So I would put on a smile and sit and talk to her about the day as if nothing out of the ordinary were happening, happy little stolen conversations all based on my religious fiction, all full of comfort and compassion, woven out of hope and desperation, belief and anger, clipped out of a positive-thinking journal and hastily glued on to life with a lie.

"How was your day, sweetheart?"

"Fine, Mom. How was yours?"

"OK. The coughing comes and goes but I—"

"We're studying the book of Romans in Bible class. I got an A on the memory quiz. Only missed a couple of words."

"That's wonderful. I knew you could do it."

Ah, that simple smile and heart-snapping fragility; it was more than I could fight, pure affection and pure truth mixed without mercy. Purity of affection, purity of truth, two more of my mother's contradictions.

Hope . . .

But I don't want to sit here writing about this right here, right now, any more than I wanted to sit on that metal-frame bed then and watch her die. I don't want to make it pretty and I don't want to make it marketable and I don't want to pretend that it's all alright now, and that I don't grieve now, that I've found some rung on the karmic ladder that justifies a second of it in the here and now.

I don't want to pretend that I don't sometimes hear a song on the radio and think, *She'll love this! I can't wait until she hears it,* before the first shock wave of reality hits the breakers and I remember that she is dead and she is gone.

I don't want to pretend, I don't want to take part in the grand social conspiracy that makes widows tell strangers on the bus that "it was his time," or makes the parents of buried children say, "Well, we're just happy we had her for as long as we did," or that in any other way makes any of us pretend that we're not furious about the double-edged broadsword of life and death, the invariable injustice of the last breath and the last heartbeat, the nagging, chronic agony of the irreplaceable that infects us all and leaves at least some part of our lives permanently and irrevocably fucked.

But that is only the way I feel tonight, nothing more. Tomorrow I will want to play again, tomorrow I will pick up the game. By tomorrow night these thoughts will look cold and strange; by to-morrow a future mercy will have been somehow connived and swin-dled out of the reality of today.

We took her to the hospital on a Saturday. Mrs. May drove the car while my mother stretched out in the backseat trying to maintain the perpendicular position that kept the fluid in her lungs from pressing against her chest; when the water tilted she could not breathe. I sat in the front seat with my Bible opened and the verses I had highlighted in yellow and red and green staring up like a blank-faced rainbow. I mirrored that face, and when they would not have faith, when they would not turn the car around, said, "Well, they'll probably only keep you for a couple of days. A couple of days, at the most."

"Scott . . ."

"Two, maybe three days. They're going to find nothing wrong with you, I'd bet on that. You'll be coming home . . . coming back . . . in less than a week."

"Scottie."

"Then we can start looking for our own place . . ."

"I think you need to understand that I am dying," she said. "Scot-tie, I am dying."

She emphasized that word—"dying"—as if she were speaking it to a very small child who didn't know the meaning. She spoke it, and then a little ripple of pain made her slip away, and she repeated it with the faded echo of a question mark, repeated it as though all of my words and faith and prayers had built up a pretense that she almost believed in, because she wanted to.

"I—am—dying."

She spoke it to convince herself.

And then she never spoke that word again.

Even later, even when we discussed funeral arrangements or my living arrangements, she would only smile and say apologetically, "We need to clear up these things—just in case anything ever happens to me."

The treatments gave her visions.

I drove after school to St. Mary's Hospital in West Palm Beach and signed in as a visitor, always agitated at the questioning over whether or not I was next of kin. She waited, swaddled up in blankets and white sheets, her face poking out and smiling with a respirator tube pinched in between her teeth.

The water came into her lungs in tides, or something like water. I could never believe that she was drowning—not in those hot, dry, bleached surroundings—but that is what she would say, that is what she would scream before they wheeled her away down the hall, the nurse's white ripple-soled shoes flip-flopping through the corridor.

They had needles that were too long, comically long, the kind Bugs Bunny would use on cartoon patients, except that these were real things, real metal, real points. The needles went into her back and drew out the water.

She refused most medications, particularly the ones that blocked the pain and affected her mind, but the slow entry of the needles had a way of opening her up to visions. We didn't call them hallucinations then. Then, they were visions.

The secretary's voice crackled out over the school intercom.

"Will Scott Peck please collect his books and report to the office."

And then the faces in the room turned halfway around, casually, eyes scanning mine, eyes full of fascination while the rest of the face struggled for pity.

Pity.

At the hospital I sat in a room filled with white-and-blue Mother Marys and Catholic crosses, waiting, praying. An old nun came out and smiled, whispered that I could come in.

She couldn't speak, I'm still not sure why. Too weak. But she gestured frantically with her hands until I found a pencil and a yellow legal pad of paper, and she scratched out her messages.

HEAVEN—TWO ANGELS, she wrote, and then tapped angrily on the pad with the pencil point.

"You've seen heaven?"

She nodded, wrote out, TREATMENT. MADE ME FAINT. HURTS, SCOTTIE.

Let me die. Why don't you come out and say it?

SAW ANGEL OF DEATH. COMING.

Why don't you let me go?

I don't want to look. I don't want to read what is written.

SAW HIM.

"Jesus?"

No, she shook her head, not Jesus.

JIMMY.

And there was a time, somewhere, when someone built a fortress for me in the sand.

Tears.

Don't cry. You can't breathe when you cry.

NOT IN HEAVEN. JIMMY IN HELL.

Let me go, Scottie.

They that wait upon the Lord shall renew their strength. They shall mount up with wings as eagles.

Some days she was as quiet and absent as a vacant white depression in her bedsheets; on others she was full of Jesus, conducting light. Joking with doctors and orderlies, flirting when the women from church weren't circling her bed, craning their necks to one side and blinking in slow motion.

"Oh, Doctor! If I still had eyelashes, I would bat them at you." But he had started crying when she said that. So he broke a rule and sat on her bed, and I left while they talked and she stroked his hand.

Her visions brought visitors from around the county, from every church where she had made new friends. They lied to the nurses, pretending to be family members, and she backed up whatever they said. Eventually, I believe, the story was that she had fifteen brothers and sisters. Others waited in the lobby or called her on the phone on days when she could speak, looking for something, a phrase or a story or a word from God that would help them believe in heaven.

Honey and Gamp believed in heaven and in hell. They drove down from Maryland and stayed at a nearby hotel. We didn't see one another often, but Honey went to the hospital every day, sat gravely by my mother's bedside sneering at the others who came.

"They've got her doped up," she sighed. "Sky high."

"She's seen the Lord," someone insisted. "She's been in heaven."

Honey slapped her Bible shut, a judge with her gavel.

"This is insanity," she said to herself in a room full of people. She looked around fiercely, with suspicion. "Charismatic in-san-i-ty."

Unconvinced, she was left to her pain. Unbelievers always suffer in the now. The rest of us procrastinate.

Rodney visited in the afternoons. First I heard the heels of his boots, the *click-clock-click*, obscenely out of place; and then there was the five-dollar aftershave and the beer on his breath. Sour.

His boots kept him away from me, over there, wholly other. He sat in the lobby and waited until I left her and passed him on the way to the elevators. Then there was a flat, nondescript nod of his head, and he would stand up, brush at the drywall on his jeans, and walk to her room.

He only made a scene once, and that was when I wasn't there. Too drunk, I guess—maybe nostalgic—he threatened her, hit her, and they made him leave. She wanted him to come back. Wanted him to hold her hand in case she died quickly while no one was looking. She wanted his hand, even though it was the same hand that had slapped her ten thousand times; maybe *because* it was the hand that had slapped her ten thousand times.

I never understand.

"I've read somewhere that it can take up to ten years," my mother said.

"What can take ten years?" I asked without looking up from my Bible.

"For grieving to end."

"Really."

"You might just be sitting in class or at work, and all of a sudden you'll have this memory that will make you want to cry. I read it. Really."

"*I* will?"

"Hypothetically. Not specifically you."

"Oh."

I kept reading.

"In case anything ever happened to me," she said and paused. "I think I'd want the opposite. I think I'd want you to remember something about me that would make you laugh."

I looked up.

"Something that would make you laugh *really* hard. So hard you'd have to leave the room and go be by yourself. And then you'd feel like I was with you for the rest of that day."

"Oh, Micheeeeelle," Laura began, and then her head fell forward, heavy brown hair covering her face and her eyes. "It's so . . ."

Here it comes.

"It's so . . ." And her voice ran up a wire, *here it comes*, *it's going to break* . . .

". . . tragic." And that *sound* was tragic, the tinkling of glass after a mezzo-soprano buildup.

"To see you . . . passing on . . ." *That* was a polite whisper. "To see you . . . so close to seeing Jesus."

"There, there," my mother soothed and glanced over at me long enough to roll her eyes and make a ridiculous face before Laura lifted her head.

"There, there," Mother said, patting Laura's outstretched hand. "It's alright."

Every church has a Laura. One of God's little gifts. Our Laura was frustrated, married—the two, in her, were somehow intimately connected—and as sweet as sugar; grainy saccharin in the sad saintly smile. Her calling, her "ministry," was primarily to the sick, although she missed few opportunities to console anyone who was in pain, anyone who was in crisis, anyone whose family secrets had leaked out through their front door.

Whenever someone recovered from an illness, there were tiny shadows at the corners of Laura's eyes that hinted at disappointment and made you feel almost as though you should apologize.

"Well," she said, sniffling. "I've volunteered to help you with the, uh . . . with the arrangements." *More whispering.*

"Really," Mother whispered back.

"Yes." And she braved through a smile that didn't quite turn up properly at the edges. "I hope that's alright."

"Oh, of course, dear."

"I had some ideas for music, and perhaps the pastor could give that one sermon—oh, I can't remember what he calls it, but it's the one with the little boy with the cat? You know? And I thought, uh, well, here are some sort of design layouts for seating?"

"How thoughtful."

"I just scribbled them out on these doilies. It was nothing. It's kind of hard to visualize, but the side areas of the sanctuary would be open, and we can move the organ out to roughly . . . here."

"Oh, good."

"Before I go any further, is there . . ." *Don't whisper. If you whisper again, I think I'll scream.* "Is there anything that you might particularly like?"

"Just one little thing, I think," my mother said apologetically.

"Whatever—you—would—like—really—honestly. It's no trouble to change anything."

"Do you think they could put some springs under my corpse, and I could sort of pop up halfway through the service? Just for a laugh?"

The room was quiet, except for the air escaping through my nose in those short wet snorts that usually hit you halfway through a memorial service or a high school graduation.

"Well, I should probably let you get some rest," Laura said, picking up her doilies.

"Of course, you'd have to plan out a way for the lid to open on cue. Otherwise, I'd just . . . sort of thump against it."

"I'll come back later, OK?"

"Then again, *that* might have a certain effect."

"I'll call you," Laura whispered, twiddling her fingers in the air in good-bye.

I don't recall Laura attending the funeral.

• • •

"We're all praying for you, Michelle."

Nothing attracted her fury as quickly as that phrase. It was an invocation to rage.

"Your prayers are keeping me here," she said to them. "I want to go home. I appreciate your help, but . . . I. Am. Tired. I'm tired, and I just want to go home."

Then they would ask about the visions, and she would tell them gently, as if they might break.

She sent everyone else from the room and asked me to sit on her bed.

The words have faded now. They are ten years old, and in the worst of those years they have been tarnished; now they are too perfect, too shiny, a chalk outline, maybe more beautiful than they really could have been, maybe not beautiful enough.

I was in heaven, she said. *And I was holding a baby.*

In heaven my hair is long again, and I can look down to see the muscles in my legs, firm and strong from running or dancing. And my whole body breathes. It takes in light, and light comes from it, peeking through the pores, but just a little, so that everyone there is always faintly shining.

And the baby in my arms is sleeping. I am holding him for someone else, someone who knows I am here alone waiting.

And then a group of women shawled in white and aqua robes, with flowers and tiaras in their hair, come running to the window, and they call in to me.

"Your son is here," they say.

So I hand one of them the baby and I start running. And oh, Scottie, I can run so quickly! Like a deer running for a stream, so fast that everything becomes a blur, blues and greens and grass and trees, all merging together and sailing by like a moving impressionist painting.

And I know in heaven where I am and where I am going.

And I come to the river that they call the River of Life, where you look out into darkness, but the darkness becomes light close to the shore, and you see seashells and goldfish and sand made from crushed diamonds under the water's stirring. And I know everyone crosses the river. Everyone who has not seen, everyone who has not seen Jesus, but still has believed.

And then I see you coming out from the darkness in a tiny boat, and you look so frightened. You don't know what is happening.

The water guides you to the shore, and then you stand up, scared to step into the water, but you do, gently, trying to find your courage. And I open my mouth to call your name.

But the sound that comes out is different, Eastern, beautiful, with rolling r's and angels' vowels, and it moves me like the singing of a choir in a monastery. It is your name, but it is your new name, given to you by God; because he gives everyone who passes the river a new name and writes it on gold or on crystal and sets it in place on the pillars of his kingdom, so that you forget who you were and begin an eternal lifetime with him.

And when you heard it, you knew it, you finally understood. And you turned around and saw me and held up your arms.

And then it was over and I was alive again.

"In case anything ever happens to me," she said on that last day, "just in case—I'd like to know where you want to live."

The question was a hard one. It slapped my face.

"Your father wants you to live with him. His wife does too."

"I don't know him."

"You could get to know him. You need to."

"I don't know him."

"Alright, what about the Mays? They care about you. You could stay with them during the school year and see your father in the summers."

"Whatever."

"Would you like to do that?"

"That'd be alright. In case anything ever happened to you."

She took my hand and filled it with something. Heat or something.

"And I need to ask one little favor from you," she said.

"Alright."

"Stop praying for me."

If there were tears shed at her funeral, I don't remember them. Nothing came out of me.

I heard someone whispering, "God, he's calloused."

That's one memory. There aren't many others.

I sat on the pew next to Lisa, who after the funeral would drive off in a car with Rodney and his girlfriend, drive "home" with them, while I would drive "home" to the Mays. They sang songs, and someone played her favorite hymn on a guitar, and a preacher warned those listening that death would come for all of us, so we had better be ready.

And I was ready, as ready as anyone in the world.

There was one moment, at the graveside, when the eulogies had been politely spoken and the mourners cried on cue and we were all supposed to quietly walk away and drive away and let the employees do the work that they are paid to do.

But I did not move, and a deacon in the church came and put his big hand on my shoulder, whispering unheard platitudes in my ear, telling me it was time to leave.

But I had to let her know that I would not have left. I would not leave. I never would have walked away, turned my back while she died alone. I would have stayed with her, lingered and prayed with her at the gates of hell if she had asked me.

And I had to let her know that I was so sorry that God had missed me with his lightning bolt, his cancer, and somehow she had paid the price for my sin. I had to let her know that I really knew, and had really known all along, that it was not her lack of faith that kept away her healing. It was my desire, my sin. It was *my* fault she was in that box, and if I could, I would have climbed in for her and let the cold dirt cover me instead. I would have and I wanted to, because I loved her as much as God loved her, and I hated myself as much as God hated me.

But then I was weak and left her there, let the Christian brothers and sisters escort me away.

s i x

My father had a way of staring at you, all gray-blue eyes with something unknown, some superior secret dancing in the pupils, a cold stare that suggested you were lacking in every imaginable category, incredibly deficient for not being him.

Or that, at least, was his image when I rode the plane from Florida to California to visit him the summer after my mother died.

He met me at the airport, and the conversation wasn't there, it just wasn't, it didn't exist. He made small talk, and I said things that instantly sounded foreign and idiotic, and we walked to his car while he chain-smoked his Marlboro cigarettes.

We hadn't even made it out of the parking lot and onto the nearest entrance to the freeway before a couple of rednecks in a truck blared their horn at him for the way he took the curve, and one of them held up his middle finger, shouted a loud, playful, stupid "Fuck you!" as we swerved around the front of their hood.

So we came to the stoplight, and there I was, buckled in and covered up in cigarette fog, and my father unbuckled his seat belt and stepped out without a word. He walked back to the truck with the two teenaged guys in the cab and knocked on their hood, motioning to them with the crook of his finger.

"You have something to say to me?"

And Christ, what he must have looked like to them, shaved head, crew cut, two-hundred-pound side of beef with a red testosterone haze burning up off of his cheeks. There was a flurry of motion in the cab, their baseball caps slipping off their heads while their mouths moved, "fuck, fuck," and they scrambled to lock the doors.

He walked back, the light already green, and no one honked their horns, not even here in California. He took his time.

"Does that happen a lot?" I asked, *inept, you idiot, why don't you just keep quiet*, and he grumbled something under his breath, but I couldn't hear him when he talked to himself or to no one—when he talks, but only under his breath.

It had been easier the year before at our first meeting, because that had all been fantasy. A comic book dream with neat boxes and balloon thoughts and a promised hero's storybook ending. I had only to follow my lines as I stood on the last paragraph of the last page. The reconciliation. My father, the shadow, prophecy, the second coming—I had always known that one day he would come to whisk me away.

He came, but what a pathetic advent it had been. The sky forgot to part, and God forgot to tell the earth to shake. Choirs of angels cleared their throats and coughed, too bored to sing. No trumpets or tidal waves. Only reality, all harshness and vulgarity, all flesh and bones and blood and life. All empty spaces between words, silence ruling over us like a merciless king, whose court jester snatched away our words and strings of thoughts before we could get them out into the air.

And worst of all, I had even been forced to consider the possibility that I was not the center of the universe.

We walked up the short driveway, stepping over meticulous rows of flowers and Maui lawn lights lined up against the trimmed edge of the lawn like little glow-in-the-dark soldiers. The beeps and whistles of video games escaped through the front window.

"I forgot they were here," he said and fished for his keys.

Two little boys, six and four, knelt in front of the television in the living room, working joysticks and staring like statues at the screen.

"Ryan? Josh?" he called, trying in vain to drag their attention away.

"Well anyway," he said, glancing back at me while he walked down the hall to hang up his uniform. "There are your . . . step-brothers or half brothers or whatever."

"Hey, guys," I whispered, walking over to them. "Nice to meet ya."

Ryan, the oldest, looked up for a millisecond, grunted, and returned to his game. Then he looked back, and his Pac-Man squealed and perished while we stared at each other. The same hair, the same eyes, my father—*our* father—chiseled into our cheekbones, the curve of our chins. Even the surprise was genetic, we had stolen his expression.

Joanne came from the kitchen with her smile, her Midwestern smile, her solid, friendly, and decidedly Lutheran smile.

"Hi! How was the flight?"

Ah, *words*.

"Great," I said, walking into the next room with her. "I sat next to a rabbi all the way from Florida."

"A rabbi?"

"Yep. Orthodox too. Temple curls and the whole nine yards. But ham sandwiches were all they had for dinner, so he couldn't eat them. And I couldn't just sit there and eat in front of him, with his stomach rumbling like the Dead Sea."

"Well, then, you must be starved! Come on, dinner's almost ready."

Joanne's world was ordered, structured, paint by numbers and connect along preordained dotted lines. The final picture, seen from a distance, she recognized as God. An easy-to-follow divinity, instead of a dictator or a measuring stick up in the heavens always judging us and always finding us wanting. A strange God.

"I see you met your brothers."

"Yeah. Quiet kids."

"Video addicts," she laughed and laid out the silverware and plates, counterclockwise, each fork and spoon lined up with geometric symmetry. "I'm glad you're here. You can help me drag them to Sunday school."

"They don't love God?"

"I don't know. Not yet."

Joanne loved her God. If you can love something that is more of a principle than a person, a matching set of principles, love and discipline, order and compassion, mixed in and blended together without confusion according to some ancient Lutheran cookbook recipe.

"We're glad you're here."

"Thanks."

"I mean both of us. Your father's glad you're here."

And I don't know what else to say about her except that she loved me and her uniforms fit her perfectly.

They drank wine with dinner, glass after glass filled and emptied, white, and my father's dark burgundy. By eight, Ryan and Josh were in bed.

Then they talked to each other or watched TV or sat together in easy silence and read. I squeezed into these patterns studiously, tried to keep the conversations alive by focusing them on Joanne or listening as my father launched into another political sermon, *you laugh when he gives the punchline*, learning from them when to turn up the volume, when to let go of the conversation, *he stares at you when you speak*, when to lean back into their Southwestern pillows and breathe.

At night in bed I relived the conversations, pretended that I had known the right things to say.

"There is no such thing as a social drinker. Alcohol will always make you its slave."

Preachers' voices filled the house during the days while my father and Joanne were at work on the base. California had a Babel of Christian television and radio stations, enough so that one could hear sermons and Bible studies all night and all day.

The promised land.

"Debauchery is a sin against the body, the temple of the Holy Spirit. If you die under the influence of that drug, with that sour sin still fresh on your lips, you cannot hope to be saved."

When I thought of alcohol, heard it decried from the pulpit, I thought immediately of beer. Cans and cans of it, piling up next to Rodney in his recliner chugging them down and belching over the sounds of *Family Feud*, then roaring in delight as if he had just made some incredibly witty observation or contributed something to the totality of the universe. Either that or I thought of Catholicism, the dark papist enemy, and the stories we were told about how Catholic priests, drunkards every one of them, sloshed out real wine to their congregations during communion instead of, as was the practice in real churches, Welch's grape juice.

But this house is like a stranger's church, with evening meditations and the drinking of wine. There is silence before communion. Even between them. Their mouths smile and laugh after their lips are red. Wine is the grace that lets strangers speak; and I will fake initiation.

"I think I'd like to try some," I said at dinner. "Try some wine."

My father raised his brow and flattened his ears back like a cat, in mock surprise.

"Well, alright!" Joanne said merrily. "You have to start young if you're going to learn to drink responsibly."

She pulled out an extra glass and filled it.

The first sip sang across the roof of my mouth like a wet bullet, left a dry and chalky impression. Carbonated vinegar with a token drop of fruit punch. I sipped at it again, then again, taking in as little as possible, then finally gulping it down when no one was looking. There. That's enough. That's finished.

But then magic began. Everything fit. From the plates and basket of bread to the pictures on the wall and the Kenmore microwave oven and my father and Joanne and I—everything had its own place, held its place, with no right angles or rough edges.

I hardly noticed the second glass of wine until it was almost gone and someone filled it again. Whenever I reached for it, it was filled. The conversation between us swelled, colored with laughter and jokes that were too clever, too perfect, too abstract to be real. We moved into the living room, and my father put on a tape of himself when he appeared on *TV Bloopers and Practical Jokes*, with Ed McMahon. I watched, amazed to see him so small, encapsulated in the TV screen, looking nervous next to the monolithic McMahon.

Nervous? Nervousness implied mortality, and that was incredibly funny. Mortality was a clown suit, red spots and stripes and a plastic nose, and it looked ridiculous on him.

Then the tape was over and there was this dragonfly buzzing in the head, and the room shifted like horizontal bars on a nervous television set. Words dried, slurred to a stop, and we sat in silence watching the news, something about brush fires in southern California and homes destroyed and someone taken to a hospital, and I started laughing, drawing strange looks, betrayed as an outsider. Funny. Funnier still. Reached for the glass again, spilled it, red wine pouring out over their *Leatherneck* magazines, *ha, ha, ha,* and dripping obscenely onto the carpet, and Joanne's hand is on my back as I open my mouth and more red wine is spilled.

Someone has taken over my body.

There is someone inside who is standing up and sitting back down and standing up again, resisting guiding hands that want to take me to the bathroom at the end of the hall. Someone is talking, angry words, and I watch two arms gesticulate clumsily, waving in the air, throwing lazy punches at nothing and at no one.

I am too much lost in this cornerless haze to care. Whoever this is, he knows what he is doing.

"Where the fuck were you?" An angry voice. *"Who the fuck are you, and where the fuck were you?"* An angry voice, and distanced. Maybe I am leaning forward to better hear it.

My father's face fades in and out, but Christ, everything is moving, nothing is standing still except the tin-voiced man inside who reels and sways and feels like an old skin flask or a kidney that has ruptured.

Then we are in the bathroom, I am lying naked in the tub with ice water slapping my face, and Joanne hovers above. It is all terrible, everything, and that is funny. Fucking hysterical.

"Wherethefuck were you, you son of a bitchwhere the fuck were you do you knowwhat happenedwhere were youyou never came."

The next morning a wave brought me in.

He appeared about noon, home early for some unidentified reason. *Joanne made you come.*

I lay on the couch and pretended to be asleep, but he was smarter than that. I could hear him in the room, and above that could feel him, could feel a cool shadow fall over my face, darker than the darkness in the room.

Joanne made you come. And what are your orders? What are you supposed to say?

"I'm leaving some carpet cleaner here on the end table," he said. "Why don't you clean the rug before Joanne gets home." A statement, not a suggestion.

I dragged my eyelids open; dry sandpaper across the lenses.

And?

Found sleep had only muted the whirlwind of motion; edges and patterns still dancing to the kettledrum between my ears, fresh pain with a decent beat.

"When I come home, later, we can talk about some of your . . . resentments."

"I don't know what I said last night, I can't remember."

"Well, we can talk about that later."

"I don't think we really need to talk about anything. Whatever resentments I have—had—I've prayed about. I've settled them."

He nodded and looked disgusted and walked away, but left a hole in the air where he had been standing that didn't close again until I heard him fumbling with his keys, stepping outside, and locking the door.

I called Mrs. May collect, her pale voice bland and reassuring. It settled the stomach.

"How are things going? Are you getting to know your father? We've been praying for you, you know."

"Last night . . . something happened."

"You don't sound good."

"I got drunk. I got really, really drunk."

"No you didn't."

"I did. I said . . . terrible things. I really blew it, I really, really did."

Her silence was a sermon; faint crackling telephone silence with the weight and burden of sin.

"Pray for me," I said. "Can we pray right now?"

But the prayer was poisoned with her disappointment and disbelief, leaking through from the "Dear Savior, we humbly beseech thee" to the "Amen," like me a weak and palsied bitter thing.

We didn't talk that night. We mumbled and stared at our plates. And that was the summer. If silence before had made us stumble, words tripping and faltering, thoughts drifting out into nothing, no sentence complete, then after the red wine it was crippling. My father sat at the head of the table like ten million other heads of other families, with a shroud of ambivalence surrounding him that no cautious conversation could ever cure, making small talk about his day, and I could think of nothing, no thing, no words with which to respond.

Even Joanne could not build a structure between the extremes. And Joanne, I thought, could fix anything.

So we became these tennis players in a tired, ancient match, the father and the son lobbing deflated balls to each other, pretense upon pretense that doesn't quite work, that doesn't quite reach, and Joanne, the mother, scurrying after each one to ease the angry silence and bring the pointless game to a close. Love, love.

When the final morning came, and my bags and Bible were packed neatly in a military fashion, and there was coffee with cream waiting on the hardwood kitchen table, and NPR's familiar voices made the morning *sound* like morning, and my father dressed early to drive me to LAX, there was a feeling swollen in our throats; or in my throat and Joanne's.

She stood on the front porch while the car warmed up and pulled away, stood there in her bright green bathrobe looking out through her Coke-bottle glasses and holding up one hand in what was supposed to be a wave but was more like a salute. A little German salute, and if life had a backup score, I guess taps would have fit. Her vision of family cracked into a thousand and one eggshell pieces, and no orders or prewritten prayers could save it.

And if there can be one traceable moment when you know you began loving someone, then there is that moment, frozen in place on the front porch in the middle of a dirty Los Angeles morning, frozen in time, wrapped up in green and looking at me through Coke-bottle glasses.

• • •

At seventeen I felt I had sufficiently searched through the past and found the answers. To everything. Which is, of course, the whole point of *being* seventeen. But when you are born again, when you are a son of God, you have a special license for arrogance, a holy dispensation. It is natural to you, it is your birthright. It is taught to you, *God's chosen one*, it is given to you by your teachers. The world you receive along with your times tables and your ABC's is that flat fundamentalist cosmology—where God, who is infinite, is infinitely concerned with your every grievance and decision and detail, from what to do with your life to which shirt to wear in the morning. And remarkably, God usually agrees with you.

And I could have lived the rest of my life like that. I might have enjoyed living the rest of my life like that.

But I loved a boy that year.

Glenn didn't belong in Florida. Not with those eyes—dark and wet and curved at the corners, Near Eastern. Olive skin melted out over this thick-muscle frame. He did not go to our school. He was different, and we didn't like different. He *made* us like him, made us love him; and he was a Baptist; and he was an American.

So the son of Allah, with his ancestors buried somewhere in sand, played baseball and wore Nikes and said, "Praise the Lord."

And it was my father's fault, the way I felt. It had to be. Because I was a son of God, a chosen one, a Christian. And no Christian would normally feel that shaking in the stomach, that tightening, that dry-mouthed lust, watching him play baseball.

Glenn's church was a graveyard. That's what everyone said. Cracked and parched and sermon piled on sermon about the length of women's skirts and how a believer should wear his hair. A man's hair should never reach his ears. And on the sides, around the temples, it should be too short to pinch. That's how Jesus really wore his hair. The Renaissance painters were liars. He didn't wear his hair like a Jew.

I went to his church on Sunday nights. Then again on Wednesdays for youth group. I lied to my pastor about where I'd been, elaborate excuses. Drew closer to him, closer then closer still. Met his family, his older brothers and beautiful dark sisters. Went to his games, oblivious to scores and innings, watched him and talked to him after he was done; strong words and compliments.

I invited him to spend the night at the Mays'. It was a hot night, so we spread out sheets on the floor and lay next to the fan.

"I like your dad," I said. "He's by far the coolest deacon at your church."

"Yeah," he said.

"You get along with him?"

"Yeah. He's my best friend."

Stars hang lower in Florida. Their light through the window gave him a glow, an aura. Blue-and-white around the edges, and his face in cobalt shadows.

"Do you have a girlfriend?" he asked.

"Yeah," I said, because I always made a point of having a girlfriend. "How about you?"

"Nah." And he sighed and stretched out like a cat. "Nah, no interest." So we talked about baseball and our fathers and youth group. He slept lightly, wrapped up in his sheet, Bedouin. And I slept well, because we did not talk about women.

But it was only admiration.

If my father had been a father, then there would be no need to feel this, no need to look elsewhere. Like drinking from a well, like drinking from my father's well—as a child, I would have been satisfied.

But he had not been a father, and Rodney had been a photograph negative of a father, and there was nothing but dirt in the well. And that was why my mouth was dry. And it was admiration that sucked away my wind, accelerated my heartbeat, and left me looking and stranded; all admiration and only admiration.

Because if it were more than that, I would have to be gay. And the sons of God are never gay. The sons of God are men.

Glenn graduated and decided against going to Bible college. Less a decision, really, more adolescent inaction that works just as well as decision. He bought a motorcycle instead of going to college.

I bought mine the same week. We bought them together. Jet black twin-cylinder Yamaha 650 Specials, with two pairs of black leather steel-tipped boots and black leather jackets to match. And I bought a Bible with gold-leafed pages and a cover made of black morocco leather. Black-strap assurance of salvation. And I cut my hair short like a marine.

After school, ashamed of still being in school, I rode to his house and twisted the engine in his driveway, revved it long and loud because his parents weren't home yet, so I could rev it and watch the neighbors mouthing obscenities behind their windows. And Glenn would roll his bike out of the garage and we would ride, purposefully, just to be seen, just to show off our chrome like the big boys who could afford Harleys. When it was dark we went home to watch Christian rock videos on cable TV.

Late in the year, we started wrestling. The first time he took me by surprise. Lunged catlike, and he smelled like sweat and oil. I was stronger, but he was fast and he wanted to win. And I did not want to win. Admiration thudded against my ribs, forced blood into areas that betrayed me, and I did not want to win.

So he lay on top of me, breathing in pants like a lion, with my legs wrapped around his legs or his back, and he gloated and boasted and put his face down on my shoulder, down next to mine, but he did not move. He only lay on top of me. And his cheek was rough, like his breath on my neck. And until summer we rode less and talked less and wrestled more.

And I loved him.

I would not have said that, I would have hurt you if you had said that.

And everything important is a choice. Like belief, like salvation. You choose what you will believe, and you *will* yourself to believe it. You choose who you will love, and you will yourself to love them. And what I chose for Glenn, what I pulled out from the crypt for him, once I knew that I loved him, was steel. Unyielding hatred and cold steel.

Because he was without excuse. In church, with his family, and his father's arm around his neck—he had a father, he needed no one and no man and nothing—he was without excuse. When he was with me and smiled at me—and the way he smiled at me, he should be more careful with his smiles—he was without excuse. When we wrestled and he wanted to wrestle as if there was love in wrestling, he was guilty and he was without excuse. That was his crime, that was my conviction, that is what I held because I chose it. Because otherwise . . .

Otherwise it was all my sin and not the sin of my father. Something inside me, some worm that had always been inside me, and not someone else's oversight or negligence. Some choice I was making every second of every day, thinking I was making the right decisions, *pray harder, fast longer, beat yourself if you have to*, but making the wrong decision, just the same. Otherwise, it was not that I had no father, it was only that . . .

Jesus, there is something wrong with me.

You learn how to hate him, to prove that there is nothing wrong with you. First, only a small hate; you make up irritations, side block him with coldness, and when he responds with coldness, you feel hurt and he is condemned. You push him away when he touches you and when he lies on you; swelling, you push him off. He does not understand, and that innocence is another reason for hating.

When you sell your bike he fades away.

His mother called to tell me he was leaving, he was joining the marines. She was throwing him a party, and she hadn't asked him, but she was so sure he would want me to come. On the appointed night, I drove to the church, sat awhile in the parking lot. Drove home alone.

A year later everyone told me, as if I would be glad to hear it, that he was back in town. He left the marines, he was no longer a marine even though he had been a good marine, and his father would not talk to him.

seven

We sit in the auditorium waiting for the spotlights to dim. There are six hundred of us, maybe more, and our excited whispers churn like a great evangelical ocean. Our notebooks and pens are in place; Bibles not far out of reach, tucked respectfully under our seats. Our hands itch to open them.

I glance over at Bill, noting the changes in him since he too received the call to enter the ministry; since the Spirit commissioned him to preach during an all-night prayer service at Bible camp. His jaw is set more firmly now, more squarely, just like his priorities. His rich black eyes scan this crowd; he is the perfect picture of a preacher already, a spiritual hawk on the lookout for sin.

"I've got a really good feeling about this," I whisper, nudging him out of meditation.

And then there is no more light. And silence in the void. Until the gigantic video screen blinks into life.

"Welcome, brothers and sisters, to the Institute for Basic Youth Conflicts!"

Applause, and the Gothard Seminar begins.

Everyone who was anyone, everyone who wanted a guaranteed place at the VIP table at the last marriage supper of the Lamb, forked out the cash and attended the Gothard Seminar.

Bill Gothard, Brother Bill, was God's man. Celibate and painfully moral, his message of spiritual authority had taken evangelicalism by storm some time in the late seventies, and one could hear his echoes in a thousand sermons preached in a thousand different churches on a thousand different Sundays. His seminars were the born-again version of EST, with devotees sitting quietly and listening hour after hour as their duties, responsibilities, sexual boundaries, and sins were all charted out neatly by Brother Gothard on his overhead slide projector.

His messages were clear and could be diagrammed easily, with points A and B and little boxed graphics for the subpoints; Christianity carved up like a sentence in grammar school. His trumpet call and trademark was authority. Spiritual authority. Vows of obedience, forgotten for centuries by Protestants, sprang to life renewed and baptized with fundamentalist flair.

But unlike the scriptures, negligently unclear on black-and-white details, Brother Gothard had the acuity to figure out for us exactly who our authorities were and how we should obey them. The outlines were clear, illustrated for us in the books we received at the door, so as to avoid any unpleasant or irresponsible independent thought.

Bitter. Those were bitter days.

The foundation for Brother Gothard's teachings was the Bible, eternal, inerrant, and preinterpreted for your convenience. If the Bible said something was true, it was true. If the Bible said something was false, it was false. If the Bible didn't mention it, it was suspect, and you'd better consult your Institute for Basic Youth Conflicts guidebook for clarification.

A mixture of Aristotelian philosophy and a bad trip on LSD, his theology left Bill and me astounded and enthralled. We had been taught all of our lives that God was immanent in the world, unseen but speaking to us through every leaf, every tree, every cloud, and every movement of the bowels, if only we would listen. But we had never heard this theory explained before so "logically."

"The scripture says that we should be like sheep," our guru told us, and we were all ready to bleat. "Sheep, of course, regurgitate their food and then redigest it."

Hmmmm, we all mused in unison. But what does it mean, what does it mean? Tell us, Brother Gothard.

He put up a slide. Cross-sectional view of the stomach and throat of a fluffy white quadruped.

"Clearly," he intoned, "what God is saying is that we should regurgitate—spiritually speaking—his word, meditate upon it, and then take it down again."

Ahhhhh, we see.

"Did you catch that, Bill?" Christ, this was good stuff!

"No," Bill said with obvious concern. "He lost me somewhere inside the digestive track. Let me see your notes."

Ardent Gothardites could quote hundreds of verses of scripture, sometimes entire books, and they had a habit of sprinkling the majestic "thee's" and "thou's" of the King James Version throughout their public prayers, their family devotional hours, and even their day-to-day interactions with heathens and other non-Gothardites, who probably thought they were either Amish or just slightly unbalanced. Bill and I *envied* their intensity, loved their smiles and their language, and before the seminar had even finished, began the task of committing the New Testament, line by eloquent line, to memory.

The word is still with me today.

Any good fundamentalist believes that a prophet's validity can be judged by the degree to which his words and teachings are offensive. Truth should be improbable, irritating to swallow like a mustard seed. That rule left no doubt, therefore, that Brother was as righteous as he appeared to be; the thundercloud of conviction rested over our heads the moment he parted his lips, and continued until his final stoic "Amen."

In between, there was a great deal of sodomy. The unmentionable sin, the sin of sins, weaved in and out of Brother's teachings with suspicious regularity; most mundane sins in some way involved or led to this one great cardinal sin.

Husbands and wives, for example, were strictly prohibited from engaging in any kind of sex other than in the procreative position, because all other positions were "by definition" sodomitic. He said he had looked it up in the dictionary, and we were accustomed to believing what is written.

Rock music was banned, even gospel music with too much of a beat, and to back this up we heard horrific stories of rock devotees who ended up writhing on the floor in flop houses, infested by demons, or, worse still by far, became involved in . . . that's right, sodomy. And Christians should not study other schools of thought or religion, particularly philosophy, because, Brother Gothard assured us with a casual wave of his hand, Socrates and the other Greeks were rampant homosexuals.

I shut my eyes and sweat, hell's flames tickling the soles of my feet, sure that if I were to pry open my lids, I would see every legitimate believer in the building turning and straining their necks to get a look at me.

"God help us all," they would suddenly howl to the skies. "A sodomite! There's a sodomite in the seminar!"

"What should we do? Brother Gothard, give us guidance! What should we do?"

And Big Brother would look out through the video screen, shaking his huge Technicolor head sadly.

"Please refer to page fifteen, subparagraph A-4, in your Institute for Basic Youth Conflicts guidebook, children."

Pages flip frantically.

"The book of Leviticus clearly mandates death by stoning for the sin of Sodom, does it not?"

And then Christians surround me, though I offer no resistance. And the followers of the Messiah wring my perverted neck and then return quietly to their seats with Christlike sneers on their angelic faces, wiping their brows and saying, "Ah, that was a close one," just as they have done throughout history.

Bitter days.

It was not sin that made Bill squirm in his seat. Not his own sin, at least.

"I think . . . I think there's something wrong with my mom," he said as we were driving to youth group together. "I think she's involved in something."

"What do you mean?"

It was a common phrase. "Involved in something." Even the best Christians sometimes became "involved in something." Record and tape clubs. Mixed dancing. Marketing schemes.

Oh, Lord. Not Amway. Don't let it be Amway.

"I think she might be gay."

Ridiculous. Lesbians, as everyone knew, were steelworkers or tennis stars, not teachers in Christian schools.

"How did you get an idea like that?"

"Come on, Scott, take a look at Shirley."

But I didn't want to look at Shirley.

She had been sick for the better part of two years. Cancer began in her breast and was removed; shattered fragments traveled through her lymphatic system, decimated her body, finally settled in her stomach and began rotting there.

Sandy talked about Shirley the way a wife becomes obsessed with an illness in her husband, taking it on, mirroring symptoms; she wrung and pulled at her hands, burst midsentence into tears that sounded a lot like guilt, then anger, then guilt again. Sounded like something more than sisterly concern. And it was alright at first, before it became uncomfortable, embarrassing.

Bill tried to be supportive and Christlike. He went to church and offered up prayers, he talked to her and about her dutifully. He answered people's questions. But you had to be warm and blind to miss the coldness in his approach, something vacant in the eyes, something hidden between the lines of clichés. Contempt.

"Your aunt?" I asked, just to say something. "What about her?"

"She's not my aunt."

Truth reared up and rattled, spread its hood. Sandy and Shirley with their pretense at family. Sandy with her meek and rouged femininity. Shirley with her starched T-shirts, boots, and blue jeans. Sandy and Shirley, and the time you snuck into their room and saw the one bed, and something sucker punched you with the implications, before the peace that passes all understanding smoothed out the wrinkles on your forehead. Sisters. They were sisters after all. And this was a very big bed.

A very big bed, and very big bullshit, but . . .

But what?

But what should *I believe?*

"Satan is just filling you with confusion," I snapped. "You should repent for even thinking something like that."

"Think so?" Bill was trying hard. Bill was trying very hard.

"That's the most terrible, disgusting, filthy sin in the world. Your mother could never be involved in something like that."

And we both stared ahead and believed.

Shirley died politely. We never guessed all that sandpaper roughness was more than a facade; she was steel to the core, dignified steel, she was the real thing. Too sick anymore to sit and smoke and talk football with her friends, she apologized—embarrassed—and retreated. A strong Southern woman, she had long before convinced herself that weakness was a limp excuse, a synonym for shame.

What she owned she left to Sandy, who was hollow, transparent, in the last few weeks. Shirley sat up in bed, arranged her finances, wrote the program for her funeral. A simple service, with piano music and tapes of Nana Moskouri, because she loved Nana Moskouri and had once gone backstage and shook her hand and Moskouri had hugged her and kissed her, and spoke to her in French.

And then there were a few words from a friend who was a former priest. Sandy had never mentioned that Shirley was a Catholic. But it was too late to argue with her anyway. They burned her body to ashes, no record of pain.

Sandy's red hair bobbed up and down in the crowd of mourners, whispering condolences, stepping aside for those who shared Shirley's blood and genes, those who had the right to say they had lost family.

She mourned, but not the way you mourn a friend. Neither was this the sorrow of someone who had lost a roommate. She sat alone and rocked in her chair with the kind of pain reserved for one who has seen half of herself severed, taken away, burned ceremoniously, and sealed into a pretty vase.

At night, when the others were gone, I went to her house and filled up empty space. Bill was not there. He knew their secret. He didn't want to, but he did. His hatred was a secret, and he guarded it at Shirley's tomb. Her tomb, displayed obscenely—he told me that much—ashes on the mantel in the box. A hand-carved symbol to him of confusion, secrets, disgrace, and some woman who had tried to be his father.

We just didn't speak.

So Sandy was alone there, in her kitchen. Alone she fished through boxes to find masking tape, packed up clothes and pictures; alone she dealt with lawyers and estate notices and the dropped-jaw surprise from some of Shirley's people—*but what about the family?*—alone with straight-backed chairs and cold sheets. And so much ice-pick silence from the saints.

She brought her journal to the kitchen table, and we sat together, talked over coffee.

"I'd like to show you some things," she said and pulled out poems, one by one. She smiled that survivor's smile while she ruffled through them, prereading every line, obviously shy, obviously censoring.

I loved her strongly and thought of God's pity.

Poems dark and rich and sweet, beautiful words about a nameless lover who was strong and dependable and the archetype of security. Standing in a door frame, naked, proud, and tight hipped. Longing and women's gardens; friction and tender milk kisses.

"You can't know what these mean to me," she said while she put some aside and distracted me with fresh coffee. "I could never show these to Bill. I love him, and he's my son. But you're like the son of my soul."

"Are these about Bill's father?" I asked.

Wasn't listening.

"I think you might be part of my family."

There *is* no pity in our God.

Just as the ancient convenant with Israel had been harsh, demanding, relentless, so we possessed and were possessed by a merciless Christianity.

It will hunt you and scent you and kill you in the name of love, the rabid hound of heaven.

• • •

What is the penalty for sin?
The wages of sin is death.
And what is the gift of God?
Eternal life for those who believe.
And what are the exceptions?
Those who pervert the natural order.
And what of them?
Eternal death . . .
Even if?
Even if they believe.

And here was another person who had loved in the wrong way, the unnatural way, the way of Sodom.

(Not my way.)

And here was another person who had been judged for her sin, according to the law.

Don't you know, some honeyed voice says, *don't you know?*

God's mercy is most clear in his rage.

He chastises the ones he loves. That's why he gives them cancer. Cancer is a caress. That's why he calls them home. To pick them up out of the shit. To get them to where they can't sin, to get them clean. Up and away. From your kind of shit.

Unless they are shit. You know, unless they don't change. Then they brought it on themselves. Then you burn.

So love incarnate had punished her for this sin above all sins by taking away the object of her twisted affections.

And the lovers in Sodom had been sucked down into hell, no matter how much they clung to each other in the final moments, no matter how convinced they were that their love was real. Just as my mother had been sacrificed for my transgressions.

Yes, it was all very clear. If you're gay you deserve to die, so God has no choice but to kill you. Or if he is gracious enough not to kill you, if he holds the angel of death at bay, you can bet your eternal soul that he will make you *wish* you were dead.

Aunt Shirley was loved and lucky. Lucky Aunt Shirley.

• • •

There is an insect in Florida, some kind of locust maybe. Smaller than a locust. More quiet; it doesn't sing. It sheds its skin in the month that we call winter.

And long past the age when it is acceptable to poke at dead birds or squirrels or snakes, long past the time when you are allowed to acknowledge your fascination with dead things, I picked up their hollowed skins, transparent like blown glass, with perfect shape to the smallest detail of legs and antennae. And I looked through them at sunlight, so that you could catch colors that were snagged in the corners and crevices of the skin, jagged ice blues and grays and yellows in the little prism of a locust.

On the day of my high school graduation, my father gave me a card. It was a standard card, a neat card, a Hallmark picture of a diploma and a cap and a bird and scrolled letters, something about taking a big new step onto a big new horizon.

True. True enough. And written down like a gospel. So the truth in those words became a gospel. The gospel according to Scott and the covenant promise, because I needed them, even though they were from no one, written to no one, and had nothing to do with him or with me.

So that summer I packed up a few belongings and left for California to live with my father.

The boys in Florida covered themselves. My boys, at least, my friends, the ones who were saved. We thought it was a sin to show our chests or our knees—a backslidden girl might be tempted to look, might let that planted seed grow and swell inside of her. So for Jesus we covered our chests and our knees until we were alone. And then we stripped and showered in the locker room where there was never, could never be, anyone like me.

I hid inside a shell with my peripheral vision and prayed silently. And learned to live with the silence of sin, the double living, coped with the cloakroom sexuality. It was at least a viable thing, a manageable misery.

But the boys in California wear their sex like cologne, like something tangible, something you smell. It's mingled in and mixed up with the blond bangs and the Coppertone tans, it travels in the molecules of the air, it burns on them and I want it to burn into me.

It is wind chimes and the breeze scraping across asphalt, the squeaking of brakes, the slapping of waves at the sea.

There is no escape.

Sex is sound. My father is silent.

He is still silent. There are no words to be spoken from the altar, from the great unknown; still uncomfortable cavities in the air, half-finished sentences hanging like icicles between us. He talks to his friends, he talks to Joanne, he talks to the goddamned cats—but he will not talk to me.

"Have you applied to a college yet?" Joanne asks.

"No, I haven't picked one."

"Hmm," he says.

"I can't decide."

"Hmm."

"Hmm," rounded like the Indian OM. Like my father's soliloquy.

Somewhere prayers are being spoken. Sandy is praying for me. And Bill is praying for me. And the brothers and sisters, the congregation of saints, just beyond earshot, beyond these sounds and smells, they are all praying for me.

And then there is Janie, and she will pray for me.

"Pray with me," she says before even asking if I am a Christian. "Would you mind? Let's join hands right here. The Spirit is speaking to me."

And she prayed in the language of my rituals, comforting phrases and soothing vowels and a believer meets a believer, draws the sign of the fish on the ground.

Pray with me.

• • •

Janie and I work in a market research center, a stupid job, they make us wear blue smocks and hold blank clipboards, and we filter out into malls and walk alongside shoppers, ask them questions about their toothpaste or their menstrual cycles, quickly and casually. Then we run back to the office with our numbers and get our money. Reconnaissance.

We meet when I am being fitted for my smock. The older woman who is our manager riffles through a cardboard box, pulling out the different sizes, holding them up against my back. No, no, wrong, too small. I offer to wear my coat and tie instead, but no, you won't fit in. Here, this one fits. Wear this.

Then the tall woman, Janie, walks around the corner with her clipboard and smiles, a thirty-something smile, too many wrinkles and handsome creases around her mouth and the corners of her eyes, mismatched with her well-moussed hair with the different-colored highlights and the neon earrings, lightning bolts or something, that bounce around her neck. And there is too much texture there, as well—so she is, I think, someone who wants to be something, some young and pretty something.

"Here," she says, touching me. "You tie them like this." And she straightens out the collar and buttons the right buttons and sticks a clipboard in my hands.

"Come on," she says, walking out the front door. "Just watch the way I do it. Just watch me."

After work, I ask her to a movie.

"Is this a date?" she asks.

"Did you want it to be?"

"No, no, no," she laughs, but extends her long arm, strokes at my chin. "I'm engaged."

The movie is simple. A young boy who doesn't know his father. He wants to be a writer. He finds a dead body.

Janie is in Bible college. A corner-lot born-again Lutheran Bible college with no accreditation. She is surrounded by little girls, she says, who want to be missionaries.

"So immature."

She lives with them in the dormitories. She is like a mother figure who borrows their clothing.

"The Spirit told me I'm going to marry him," she says.

"Who?"

"My professor. My fiancé."

"He proposed to you?"

"No. But he knows. You can tell. I can tell these things. The Spirit tells me."

At work our efficiency drops, we smuggle our New Testaments in the pockets of our smocks and we read in the alcoves in the mall. We sit on the benches with our clipboards and exchange notes, talk of heavenly things. Sometimes she sits too close to me.

"I can tell you're called of God," she says. "Are you going to go to seminary?"

"Yes. I think. In the spring, maybe. I've sent out my applications."

My paychecks disappear in the gospel bookstore in our mall. Reference books, music tapes, the ropes I cling to in Babylon. I dream of white collars, stained-glass windows in my office, sinners in crisis, of going to seminary.

"So," my father said at the dinner table. "Do you want to meet Clint Eastwood?"

"No, no thanks," I said, because that was my response to anything he offered.

"Suit yourself."

His billet with the corps landed him in odd jobs, strange positions. Since his most recent promotion, he had been working as a technical advisor on films. He had an office in L.A. with a view of the city; the walls were covered with marquees of military movies and one framed picture with a silhouette of a marine and a little Asian girl.

"When I tell people I served in Vietnam," it read, "they always ask me how many people I killed. They never ask how many people I saved."

"*Heartbreak Ridge*," Dad announced one night.

"What's that?"

"My new script. It's an Eastwood film. Based on the Grenada invasion. Sort of. Not really."

"Hmm," I said, feeling his excitement, slapping him back with indifference, slapping him back.

"DOD's giving them shit about it. Historical inaccuracies, they say."

"Really."

"They should just leave it alone. It's a hell of a movie."

That night I read the script. Blood and fire and honor to the highest possible exponent, and I love it with everything that is a man about me. There is always something inside a man's gut that wants to put on a uniform and die for something. And you love it because it is unrehearsed and it comes naturally.

And you hate the part of you that stiffens when you read about these men, these Hollywood, *Heartbreak Ridge* marines. Marines who pause in combat to talk about fucking each other. Just kidding. Just a joke. Just a saying.

"Fuck me."

And the Hollywood words soured my patriotic surge of testosterone, mutated it, transformed it from the proud and noble battlefield to some dark corner of a possible world, some seedy sweaty tropical night with Clint Eastwood planted squarely on top of me.

Fuck. Me.

"You have a crush on me," she says over the plastic-topped table at Denny's. The waitress has given up on our leaving and just left a pot of coffee. Janie's face is a contortion, she is smoothing a bee-pollen cream, a yellowish cream, into the pores of her skin while she speaks.

"You definitely have a crush on me. I can tell. I can tell these things."

She stops with the cream and smiles.

"Age differences are no big deal."

God is always talking to Janie, and she is always redefining things. Yesterday, she was still engaged.

"Then the . . . *jerk* . . . walked right past me. I was at school and stopped to talk to him, and he just kept walking, as if he didn't know anything. He can forget it. It's off."

"I thought the Spirit said you were getting married."

"Scott," she chided sweetly, as if I were thirty years younger, instead of only fifteen. "Free will counts for something. And quit looking at my breasts."

"What? I wasn't . . ."
"You definitely have a crush on me."

"I'm taking Greek," Bill says on the phone, and I say "Congratulations" even though I am as embarrassed and angry as he wants me to be.

"So," he says, "what are *you* up to?"

"I'm working in marketing," I exaggerate, but all I am really saying is "I'm not as good as you are. I'm not studying Greek." Greek is the language of God. When God wanted to write a book, he wrote it in Greek. When God thinks, he thinks in Greek.

"Whatever happened to you?" Bill asks. "Why aren't you following God's direction?"

It's called a prick. When a brother nudges you, hurts you to get your attention, when a believer tells you something true and you bristle at it because it stings like a bitch, it's called kicking against the pricks.

"I know, I know," I say. "I know I should be in Bible college."

"So why don't you come back home?" he says, and I love that word. "Come to Palm Beach Christian! We'd be in school together again."

"I wanted this to work."

"With your dad?"

"Yeah."

"How is he?"

"I don't know. I don't know him. He doesn't want to know me."

"Well," Bill said, after a long pause. "He *is* unsaved, after all."

The tuition at Palm Beach Christian was as high as most Ivy League schools. To earn a degree that, with a little charisma and a knack for winning souls, could make you godly *and* rich, they made you pay.

The student loan department informed me that Florida's laws could be used in my favor.

"If your mother died and your father was noncustodial, you could qualify as an orphan," she said.

"Are you sure about this?"

"Yeah."

I guess enrollment was a little low.

"So you'll be leaving us," Joanne said.

"Yep. In December."

"Going to Holy Roller school, huh?" My father. "Let me guess: the L. Ron Hubbard Institute of Airport Evangelism? What's this going to cost me?"

"Nothing."

"Scholarship?"

"No. They say I'm an orphan." And I waited for some kind of response.

"So, my son is an orphan." He laughed. "I can't wait to tell my friends."

Neither of us knew I had been misinformed. He would ultimately have to pay.

"You realize that I'm a virgin," Janie said while we sat in my car. I moved my elbow away from hers, folded my arms across my chest.

"I figured you were. You've never been married."

We had twenty minutes before the next movie. It was too cold to stand outside, too hot inside the car.

"Are you?" she asked. "A virgin?"

"Of course."

She nodded, watched people outside. There was something desolate in her that one night, some hint of fragility or depressed humanity. Something like the silence of the Spirit, an absence of fresh visions.

"That's unusual," she said. "For a man, I mean. Even a Christian."

"Guess so. In California, maybe. These guys here, even the Christians. They're so . . . ungodly."

"I suppose Southerners are all saints."

"No, just simpler. Is it getting hot in here?"

I checked my watch, held it to my ear as if something were wrong.

"That's very admirable," she said, and she was still looking away. "Your commitment."

"Thanks. We really should get in, now."

Silence while I rattled my keys.
"Or are you just gay?"

No one in the parking lot needed to walk into the theater to see a show.

I stormed around the car, first in one big circle, the air just cool enough to make me huff out smoke like a dragon. Then I walked away, then started running, then came back slowly, a hand brushing hard through my hair like an angry man.

Janie opened the passenger side door and hissed out at me.

"What are you doing?"

"GAY?" I bellowed, then lowered my voice, answered in a hiss. *"Gay?"*

"I'm sorry," she said. "Just get in the car."

I ran toward her and she slammed the door.

"What is your problem?" I called in through the glass.

"Just get in," she mouthed, but I moved to the front of the car, to the hood, and began tapping on it with the key.

"What, Janie? What could you possibly be thinking? What do you all *want with me?*"

She locked the doors.

Janie's penance was long. Her tears accomplished nothing except a softening of my voice. Softened words that cut deeper into her until she held her cream-soaked hands up in the air and turned her head away and lowered her chin as if to ward off blows or hide.

"How could you even think such a thing? You're wasting yourself, you know. You're just frustrated with this whole Spirit-talking-to-you thing. That's the whole problem. You're frustrated because you're in your thirties and you can't get a guy. That's the whole thing. You can't have sex, and that's the whole thing."

"What do you want me to do? Why are you so . . . *fucking* . . . *mean to me?"*

"I'm not being mean." Speak softly. "I'm telling you God's truth. You're just fighting, you're just kicking against the pricks."

"It's not true."

"It is. And you know it." And now there's pity. Aching, saccharine pity. "You're just rebelling. You're in sin. Sexual sin in your heart,

Janie. Don't tell me you don't think about it—having sex. With men. You do and you know it. You're in sin. You're in terrible sin."

"Stop it. Shut up. Stop."

She pulled Kleenex out of her purse, a tight white ball, smeared with it at her face, smeared off her lotions and her creams, wet it with her tongue and took off her lipstick.

"What do you want me to do?" she said, tired and embarrassed. "I'm sorry. I'm so sorry. I've already said I'm sorry."

"I want you to come and meet my parents."

I took Janie over to meet my dad and Joanne on a Friday night. She wore a miniskirt, leather I think, showing off every dangerous and well-preserved inch of her long legs.

"Pleased to meet you," my father said, and his face scrunched, his eyes narrowed, visually verifying her age.

"How do you do?" she said.

Joanne covered her surprise with smiles. "Would you like to stay for dinner?"

"Sure," Janie said.

"Oh, we really can't, can we, Janie?"

"No, well, I guess not . . ."

"We've got to get to, uh, to the movie."

"Oh, right. I forgot about that."

Are you catching this, Dad? Are you catching all this?

"Well, maybe some other time," Joanne said.

I'm fucking up my life, Dad.

"Yes." And Janie shook her hand. "That'd be nice."

And it's all your fault.

California nights are cool, sometimes cold, but I have left the windows open. There is no sound inside this house, not now, not ever.

You can freeze anything, Dad. Even hatred.

I am no stranger to loving myself in this way, resisting, resisting, then yielding to my own cold hands, sliding downwards as if they know what they are doing.

Afterwards I can pray.

Afterwards I can pray to the true God, beg his forgiveness and restraint, do not kill me yet, O Lord, tomorrow I will do better than I have done today.

Better than tonight. But tonight I worship other gods in this iced shrine, their images are real, desire compressed, expanding, the dreaded but needed explosion, that one sweet guilt-free millisecond of release.

Before the Holy Ghost crouches low by my bed.

But tonight. Tonight, the pain of losses, all of these sad and pathetic attempts at healing, all of these prayers and days of fasting and midnight confessions are killing me.

So I reach into my mind and conjure new dreams. Goddesses in gossamer, new things. Women like the women I know I should desire, I can desire, I must desire, and shoot them up onto an inner screen. Licking their lips, wanting. Wanting me.

Nothing.

I make the puppets reject me, turn away, try to hide. That is what men like. Still nothing, not so much as a tightness in the stomach or a trip in the heartbeat.

My hand works furiously, I am insulted by my body's failure to respond, by its attempted retreat, I know I can be like other men, I know I can make this happen. And if I can make this happen once, I can make it happen again and again and again until it becomes natural, until it fits and drives the men away, and then I will take these new feelings, then I will take this healing and step with it out into light.

The strokes become pumping, driving, I am pounding into myself, further offended by this *fucking crying, stop it, you little faggot, stop crying*, but God demands this, this violence, God demands it, and it only ends when I know I am bleeding.

"Well, so much for my career."

My father's face had that mixed-up, can't-decide-whether-to-laugh-or-cry schizophrenic smile quivering down around his chin.

"Didn't think it would go this far."

Heartbreak Ridge was on the evening news.

"The movie that's too tough for the Marine Corps," the reporter's voice teased over scenes from the film, Eastwood's stone-handsome face.

"What's happening?" I asked him. "You look nervous." Human, are we?

"The DOD ordered changes in the script."

"And?"

"And I forgot."

"Yeah, right."

"Now all hell's breaking loose. I was supposed to pull support until they made the changes. I couldn't."

"You blew your career for a movie?"

He leaned back against the counter uneasily, the wine in his glass swishing dangerously close to the sides.

"No. I blew my career for a point of honor."

And when he said that word, he had a hollowed-out locust gray in his eyes.

It's all a question of honor, everything.

Honor is your word, it belongs to you, if you love or are supposed to love a military man. It's the force behind reconnaissance relationships, when you dart in and try to make a connection before the next thing explodes and you get cut by all the shrapnel flying around. If your father is red-white-and-blue and wrapped up in a shroud of khaki green, honor is *your* word, the key to your father's heart.

It doesn't take much. The igniter switch can be the smallest thing. Because colonels, even good colonels, when they don't have orders coming down from above? Or when they can't find the regulation in a book? Well they've still got to pick a point and draw a line. They've just got to do it on their own, without any guidance.

So then there is the entrenchment, digging in of the heels, defending the murky ground of . . .

Honor.

Defending honor; and loving while being a man.

There is nothing harder in the universe than loving while being a man.

And most sons of most of these men would give anything, any great or small thing, to become just once enough of a priority or a prize to be won, to be encompassed in the point of honor. And the day when you realize that that is simply never going to happen, well that is the day of the testing of *your* honor. Loving your father even if he is a man.

When I left, when I got into my car to go to Bible college, to go home—there was actually this one cracked second when my throat was tight and he held me stiffly and quickly and roughly and awkwardly and said good-bye. Then there was this one second when I wanted to say, "I *do* love you," but didn't because I thought I might cry.

Doctor Campbell should have been a rabbi.

He should have been a rabbi and he wanted to be a rabbi deep in his heart of hearts, as anyone with eyes to see could tell you. It was only some cruel twist of fate that destined him to be born a Gentile and a Christian.

He was a middle-aged man with a proud round stomach that hung out over the front of his pants—but it made him look solid instead of lazy or weak—and a thick mustache that he stroked when deep in thought, as if it were a misplaced temple curl. He had studied for more than a decade before becoming a biblical studies professor, and his love of loves was the Old Testament.

Classical Hebrew could almost make him swoon. He held the difficult words in between his teeth and rolled them forcefully off his tongue, lingering over the nuances and deeper implications of every syllable, every vowel. He talked with wide reverence about rabbinical scholars, men who could hold the Law in their hands, choose a letter on the first page, drive a needle through it, and then tell you with perfect accuracy every letter the needle hit on its way through the book. They were men of learning, men of the Law, men of the book. Men like Doctor Campbell, although he would have thought it blasphemy to admit it—him with his love of the book of books, and words and scholarship sizzling around him like an aura. Doctor Campbell, my rabbi.

• • •

"You have to look around corners," he said and leaned back in a squeaky metal chair that ached and chirped and rocked. His was one of the smallest offices on campus, although he had the best degrees. He filled it with pictures, especially of Noah's ark, his favorite story, and he had one of those curio collections in wood and glass of animals and arks; and I think it was raining that day, which was too perfect, because with him I was safe and his cubicle was a nest that protected us from the waters above.

And this, by the way, is admiration.

"You're thinking one-dimensionally."

"Uh-huh," I said, no idea what he meant. But he knew that, he knew everything.

It began with Genesis in Hebrew class, when someone made some reference to the creation story and Doctor Campbell said, "Which creation story?" and we all sat very still and very quiet, thinking he wasn't supposed to say something like that.

"There are two of them," he said. "At least two."

And there was this *thud*, *thud*, *thud* in my throat.

"One in chapter one, the other in the second chapter. Two different stories, two different sequences of creation, written in two different forms of Hebrew. But I'm rambling." And incredibly, he kept talking.

"There aren't supposed to be two different stories." And I stood in the door of his office, angry and wet and accusatory. "Not if God wrote them."

And we talked about whether or not God writes books.

This boy is praying.

He is on his bed with his eyes closed and his hands folded in front of his face like a mantis. And he believes Someone is listening.

"This is Genji," the woman from admissions had said, grabbing my arm in the hallway. "He's our international student."

"Pleased to meet you."

"Genji is from *Ja-pan*," she said, whispering the final word.

Genji came to America for a college education and to learn how to surf. His parents, Japanese versions of sixties radicals, had gone to great lengths not to weigh their son down with the traditional educational expectations that lead some Japanese students to slit their wrists in warm showers.

So Genji and his parents sat down in their microscopic apartment and labored over brochures and pamphlets about colleges in America; decided on a few strong possibilities, schools with good academic standing and interesting programs. Palm Beach Christian was bubble-gum scholastics next to the other institutions, but it had a great brochure, high-gloss photos of palm trees and white sand beaches and, I think, the surf. And the decision was made.

I helped him move into our apartment, and we went through the usual routines and small talk, the polite yet mercenary dividing of drawer space.

"So, when did you receive the Lord?" I asked. Genji's English was good, slow, so when he scrunched up his face, puzzled, I thought he had misunderstood.

"Jesus," I reiterated, pointing skyward, then to my chest. "How long have you been a Christian?"

"I'm not a Christian," he said pleasantly and pointed to his own heart. "Buddhist."

There are some heretics who have suggested that religion, like any idea or living thing, is susceptible to growth and to change.

These same doubting Thomases with Ph.D.'s claim that ancient peoples moving about Asia and Europe carried their beliefs with them along with their mule packs and tent pegs and sheep—and that their thoughts blended in with their new geography, took on new hues and tones, and became new ways of looking at things.

But we know these are lies, because we have listened to missionaries.

"The people of northern Frakistan still cling stubbornly to their old beliefs."

Who was that woman? The shrill one from Frakistan. She spoke to us and passed the collection plate twice, as if *we* were the savages.

"The hardest barrier to overcome is the . . . similarity . . . of some of their thoughts to the true faith."

And then she paused, shook the enormous bun of hair on her head.

"This is because Satan planted lies in ancient places to confuse later generations. He gave them stories about virgins giving birth to God—blasphemy!—because he knew that Jesus was coming."

Stubbornness and unbelief.

"We entered the village close to midnight."

Another soul winner.

"Negroes were sitting around a campfire. 'We've come to tell you about God,' we said in Frakistanian.

" 'He was just here, sitting with us,' the chief said in English. 'He heard you were coming and decided to leave.' "

If a tribe or a nation refused to accept Jesus and stand in the middle of a pond and get dunked three times for the Father, Son, and Holy Ghost, it was never, ever, the failure of the missionaries. It was stubbornness and unbelief, those two words always in a pair, always linked like cars on a train.

If you weren't convinced, it was because you stubbornly clung to your unbelief. But you really knew. You really knew you were wrong.

And so God was wasted on the nations. So many missionaries, so many little Christian pearls trampled by the swine.

We worshiped with our own kind, married other Christians, associated only with other Christians, even shopped in stores owned by good people, by Christians. We had our own yellow pages, *The Shepherd's Guide*, with hundreds of convenient listings.

I had never met someone who wasn't a Christian. And I didn't want to.

• • •

"I, uh, don't know anything about your religion," I said.

He tried to explain, slowly, the concept of Buddhism. He tried to explain, but who was listening?

"But what about death?" I asked, interrupting, because that was the standard way to begin a conversion. "Do you know where you're going when you die?"

He laughed.

"Some people say you go across a river in a boat." And he rolled his eyes. "But I do not think that. That is for children."

"I don't think this is going to work," I said. But I said it quickly, and he didn't understand.

And behind all that, there was his life.

I like him.

Genji's father prayed in temple every morning, surrounded by so much believing. His mother cooked and cleaned and taught her children to live by the Way.

I really like him.

Yes, his mother must have loved him. She taught him to tie his shoes. She dressed him up in uniforms for school, first short pants, then long. And helped him with his homework.

"What do we look like to you?" I ask him.

"Big and loud and pale," he says. He's funny.

So he loved her too. As I had loved my mother, maybe even in a similar way. He questioned, and doubted his parents' beliefs, except that he didn't bleed so much when he threw them away.

"Well," I said meekly, because in all the familiar small talk I was always forgetting to witness, "Jesus still loves you."

"Thanks," he said. "But I don't really believe. In Jesus."

So it would take time. He was still faking. I would give him time to decide to believe.

He already believes.

I would give him some time; and then, after that, he would have to be the enemy.

• • •

"Are you saying that you've never accepted Jesus as your personal Savior?" Buddy Knox had his Bible in one hand, and his other hand was balled up in a tight white fist.

I heard his voice from the hallway and had to squeeze past the preacher boys who had surrounded Genji's bed. He sat like a lotus-flower statue, caught, I guessed, midmeditation, his secret now the center of a jihad.

"Buddhist," he said, his face tight.

"You worship Buddha?" Buddy exhaled as if sucker punched.

"No, worship's not right . . . Buddha was a teacher. A man."

"*Jesus* is the answer, man," said Buddy. "If you died tonight, do you know where you would go?"

"Die? Tonight?"

"Hell, my friend." And the boys humphed and nodded in chorus. "You would burn in hell."

And then the crowd backed away from Buddy, who sat down gently on Genji's bed. It's a holy experience, watching a brother go in for the kill.

"There's only one way out," he said, smiling sadly. "Genji, would *you* like to accept Jesus?"

"No."

Then there was a pause that Jesus could have been crucified in.

Buddy stood up and backed away. His spiritual groupies followed in single order, past me and out our door.

"Thank the Lord he's your roommate," Buddy said to me. "God! These new cults are getting out of control! There oughtta be laws."

In the silence of our little room I sat down on my bed and just stared at him. He leaned back, arms folded, tired of being stared at. Jesus, who had been no more to him than a few pages in a social studies textbook, was suddenly becoming a powerful figure, a familiar name.

Jesus Christ was the main reason no one here would be spending much time with him, no one would help him with his English, and certainly no one would teach him how to surf.

"So you believe that?" he asked. "You believe I'm going to hell?"

An inquisitor with white-hot irons up my ass couldn't have asked for a more painful confession. Not at that moment, not when the scribes and pharisees, my brothers, had just trudged from the room, showing me what a big, braying jackass I must look like to anyone who had the audacity to believe in God but believe in him differently.

"No," I said. And at that second, with that one word, according to my religion, I cast my soul and salvation to the wind.

Sandy is good.

She is good, good, good to me.

When I need her den for sulking or pacing, or when I need a quiet room to pray, she is my home. She checks in on me and makes me lasagne, and it doesn't matter that I am almost twenty, and she doesn't notice that when I talk to her she is not really my mother, because she is good, good, good to me.

Sandy's home has always been clean, but never this kind of clean. Now the books on her shelves are arranged by descending height, her windows are sparkling, her carpet hums with dustless static energy.

She must be in love, she can't fool me. Her red-rose cheeks and her dancing little green firefly eyes have betrayed her.

She has a new friend too—a woman, Karen, but if she knows the name of Sandy's new man, well, Bill says she isn't talking. I joke with her usually, but tonight we are only talking.

I'm trying to escape the confusion and the shower smells of the dormitories, the enormous spires of the college church terrorizing and all the pictures of Jesus so cold and monochromed. When I arrived she was cleaning up after dinner—a dinner for two with candles and wine.

"Had company tonight, did we?"

"No, no, not really. Just a friend."

"A male friend? A, dare I say . . . *boy*friend?"

"No, just Karen."

"Oh, well. That's boring."

We sit in her den on her thick patterned cushions, and it will be a good night, because she's sharing her poetry.

Then from nowhere the devil slips in.

"Sometimes I wonder about things," she says, her gaze unfocused. "For example, I have a friend who's gay."

That's nice. And I have Beethoven's Fifth pounding in my eardrum.

"Really?"

"Yeah. She's a Christian, she goes to church every Sunday. She goes to our church. God, if the brothers knew, she'd be out on her ear."

"Yeah. Yes, she would."

"What do you think about that—about people being gay?"

What do I think? What do I think, Sandy-who-is-supposed-to-be-good? I think: conspiracy. A friend, huh? You have a gay friend. I don't have any gay friends.

"No one knows she's gay," she says.

"She might be surprised."

You, the mother figure, the replacement, the stand-in, the double. She knew, after she was gone, I would look to you, and here you are now, everything I hate. Yes, yes, I know: love the sinner, hate your sin. But when you are the sin, when it is this sin, when it is so much a part of you, you are only the enemy. Another enemy.

"I think . . ."

The enemy who taught me history and grammar and first asked me to write you a story.

"I think that life can be a pretty lonely, cruel place," I said.

The enemy who put Dickens in my hands, Oliver Twist, *another orphan, and opened up a universe with safe pages.*

The enemy who has listened. Soft ears. The enemy who never talked much about Jesus but taught me about Jesus through her actions, her mercy; God's compassion. So this is how you learned compassion.

"And if you're lucky enough to love someone," I said, "and have them love you back, you should count yourself blessed."

I love you, but God says you are the enemy.

"Not everyone feels that way," she says.

"God is wrong."

In the dormitory no one was home. I stripped down, stepped into the two-by-two stall we used for a shower, and turned on the water. A battlefield, mortars and shells exploding in every direction.

So I had finally met a homosexual. That's what one looks like? And I was the son of her soul, she had said. She had promised. My family.

A family that loves in a way that makes you dead. Stone-cold damned and dead. An outcast in this world, French toast in the next. Something so terrible that even the saved and the unsaved can agree. They tell you to change, they tell you to go to counseling, they tell you to fast or to pray or to find the right woman.

I have done all of that.

Constriction in the muscles, dizzying, blurring my vision. I turn the faucet to hot, then hotter until it scorches the skin. Then turn the water cold, ice cold, and crouch down in the shower, and the shock brings everything back into its place, clears my head for a millisecond before I make the water hot again.

eight

Tag-team preaching.

Once a year the Holy Ghost came down on three young men who were studying to enter the ministry, during tag-team preaching. The idea was simple and allegedly inspired: each preacher-to-be delivered a fifteen-minute sermon, after which a buzzer went off, and he had better have made all of his points and convicted enough sinners, because his time was up. Then the next contestant ran to the stage, slapped the hand of his predecessor, and commenced with his sermon.

Bill and I wanted invitations so badly we salivated every time we glanced at the church calendar.

The preacher boys were usually a little rough around the edges, missing the finesse that, we were assured, comes only with experience and prayer—but what they lacked in style they made up for in intensity. Bring your earplugs. God can sound rough through a novice channel.

Winners won nothing except the admiration of the congregation and the pastoral staff—but in our tight world, recognition was status, and status was everything. And if your sermon blew the doors off the back of the church and toppled the pews, those pats on the back might just land you a pastoral internship.

Tag-team preaching was a hell of a show.

One night, one of those nights when you could die right then and there and be perfectly happy about it, Doug, our youth pastor, invited Bill and me to speak. We accepted politely and maintained our composure until safely in the church parking lot, where we proceeded to whoop and yell, and congratulate ourselves, *"Yes! Yes! Yes!"* until our throats were sore and our heads were light and our palms hurt from all the high fives.

I suppose I should have hesitated. But the pulpit was the center of the universe; I never wanted to be anything but a preacher. And even as my belief system rumbled internally and threatened to explode, the thought of stepping into the shoes of my childhood heroes and seeing the world from the other side of the altar was too much to resist.

I prepared for weeks, planning and replanning the sermon, arranging the notes Pentecostal style: a few sparse points with lots of room in between for the Holy Ghost to say whatever was on his mind. I drove out to the woods in central Florida, found a secluded grove, and practiced my sermon again and again while the sun quietly melted down, preaching the word to squirrels and sparrows and palm trees.

And doubts grew small and almost inconsequential in the excitement and the prestige, my own "sins" transparent and short lived, overlooked in the rush to expose the sins of others—I was the vehicle of judgment, temporarily immune from God's wrath.

And I knew I could preach and liked myself when I preached, because I was not myself when I preached.

We are only happy when we are outside ourselves. And that exhilaration, that transcendence is a given when you are not yourself, in the most literal sense. When you are someone else, you are some *thing* else, you are a musical instrument, yes, that is what they taught us in school, *you are violins waiting for the Master's touch. If you surrender, the Holy Ghost will pick you up and make beautiful music come from your lips.*

I had heard sermons delivered by Lutheran ministers, Methodists, and others "infiltrated and compromised" by reason and logic, and wondered if they were awake, much less experiencing the flow of rapture and emotion, the heightened helpless awareness when the Spirit of God fills your lungs and makes your fists pound the pulpit. When the world is sick and, for one second, *you* are the man with the antidote. You cannot believe that you might be wrong, you cannot believe that you are not the chosen one.

• • •

When I ran to the platform, slapped Bill's hand, and opened my Bible as the audience cheered, there was nothing in the world that was out of place.

The building of excitement in a sermon is an art form, revving the congregation like a motorcycle engine. You want souls to be saved, sinners convicted, and the devil making a hasty retreat, pointed tail tucked between his legs. If you lose your train of thought, a string of "Hallelujah's" can temporarily fill in the void; and if all else fails, you can always begin speaking in tongues, and only a charismatic with low self-esteem will ever admit that he was not spiritually attuned enough to get something out of it.

"Where is God?" I bellowed and let the church fall silent. *Timing. Watch your timing.*

"God . . . is where people are suffering."

A hearty "Amen!" from the front row foreshadowed success.

"He didn't see a world full of pain and say, 'I'll just stay up here, out of harm's way.' No! He came down to us." And at this I kneeled, holding out my hands. "He knelt, he took on a human frame, he humbled himself in the dust from which he had formed his fallen race, and said, 'Come unto me, all ye who are weary and heavy laden, and I will give you rest.' "

"Amen's" in abundance.

Good. A good start. Now a little conviction.

"Do you know who will enter the kingdom of heaven?" I thundered. "I'll tell you. Not the pompous, arrogant churchgoers who put on fancy clothes once a week and pretend to love God. No, that type winds up in hell. The ones who will find a place prepared for them at the marriage supper of the Lamb are those who do as Jesus did. Those who clothe the poor, feed the hungry, heal the sick."

We talked often of the social duty of Christians, although, in a toss-up, a new sanctuary or choir robes or a new office for the pastor got precedence over feeding the poor or the sick. Still, it was standard sermon material.

"Which category do you find yourself in tonight?"

Another pause.

"What kind of Christian are *you?*" And the question was a hiss, a whisper.

And the inner sermon began. A private message came from nowhere, or from someplace deep inside. It raged, it filled up my ears,
it pounded in my chest, it would not be ignored.

"Which kind of Christian . . ."

A whitened sepulcher.

*You're a whitewashed tomb, nothing more; so clean, so pure on the outside,
with your smug smile and your industrial-sized Bible. So very spiritual, so
self-assured, so proper, and so predictable. But take a look at your insides,
my friend. A house of corruption, a tomb full of dead men's bones.*

Shut up.

I pushed the words away, irritated, and focused on the crowd.

"When you look in the mirror, who do you see looking back at
you? Someone decent? Someone honest? Someone kind? Or do you
see a lie, pretension in fine church clothing, the mouth of Judas
poised for the final kiss? If Jesus were here now, in human form,
would he associate with you?"

If Jesus were here . . .

*But he is here, inside. Painted up like a harlot, words of self-righteous
men like yourself crammed into his mouth, mocked and ridiculed by your
pretense at following in his footsteps, carrying on in his name.*

"If Jesus were here tonight . . ."

*If Jesus were here tonight and walking around on human legs, would he
be sitting here listening to you? Or would he be somewhere else, with other
people, other outcasts and victims like himself . . . ? Wouldn't he really be
out among the lost, the lonely, the outcasts, instead of sitting here soaking
in pretty words and air-conditioning with you and the other pharisees?*

Sweat struggled through my pores, my heart pounded like a kettledrum, and I kept my mouth in motion.

"Sin is everywhere! Homosexuals, adulterers, hordes of demonic
religions! They are taking over our society! Where are the warriors
who can stop their advances?"

"Amen!"

*Look out at these faces, Judas. What about them? What about the young
faces, some of them hiding secrets as terrible as yours, secrets that would make
you and the other true believers cut them off from the Body of Christ as if
they were an infected limb.*

"America is a Christian nation! A nation for Christians!"

I was getting desperate. This was too typical, too common, weak.

"Amen!"

What about the hope in their eyes, searching for something, some shadow of acceptance, some portrait of the outcast Messiah who could accept them as they are, loving without favor, without discrimination?

"Hell is waiting for those who do not heed our message! Hell is closer than you think!"

"Hallelujah!"

You suck the hope out of them quickly enough, don't you? Just as it was drained out of you? Does it make you feel better? You pump them full of the same poisons, you rip up their fragile faith, you go into heaven and then slam the door in their faces.

"There is no room in the kingdom of heaven for those who do not believe. And there can be no room for them in a Christian America!"

"Preach it, Brother!"

What are you thinking, Iscariot? That if there is a heaven, that the wounded, the different, the little ones would be sent away, and you would be welcomed in?

"Hallelujah!"

Don't—count—on—it.

But then the buzzer rang, and I could tell by the applause that I had won.

Doug called me into his office.

"I'm impressed," he said, tapping his pen on his desk and smiling boyishly. "Your sermon was really anointed. But then I've always believed that you had the call of God on your life."

"Thank you, Pastor."

"I think it's time to promote you in the ministry—move you up the ladder, so to speak."

"I don't know . . ."

"We have a lot of areas with needs that you could fill. It would mean added responsibility, but I think you're ready, and with a little guidance, we . . ."

If Jesus were here . . .

"I don't believe in God."

"I'm sorry . . . ?"

"I don't believe in God anymore. At least not the kind of God I've always believed in."

"When did this happen?"

"I don't know. Slowly."

Doug moved closer, wheeled his office chair next to me, put the pastoral arm around my shoulder.

"This has to do with your mother, doesn't it?"

Bastard.

"In a way."

"Talk to me."

"The scripture promises healing, doesn't it? The book of First Peter: 'by his stripes, we are healed.' "

"Right."

"Or Mark: 'whatsoever you ask in my name, believing, you shall receive.' "

"Well, *believing* is the key word."

The key word. The missing key. My mother lacked faith, she misplaced her key. If she had had enough faith—if only she had had enough—she would be walking around today, she would have been sitting in the audience last week when I preached, she would have gone to heaven years from now, as a saint, instead of as a failure.

Doug lowered his head, running through lists of replies. For a Pentecostal preacher, this topic was a theological minefield. He expected it from outsiders, but not from one of the sheep.

"We can't understand everything that God—"

If Jesus were here . . . "We can't understand everything that God chooses to do, and we'd better not question him. I know the answers too. They just don't work anymore, Doug," I said, committing the cardinal sin of calling him by his first name. "First it was her faith that was defective, now I suppose it's mine. Now it's me. Maybe the whole thing is defective."

"I can understand you doubting certain doctrines, you've been through a lot. But to question the existence of God . . ."

"I don't question his existence. I just don't think you—or I—know much about him."

"God," he said, anger a slow burning bloom, "God speaks to us through his *word*, Scott. Through the scriptures. You remember the scriptures?"

Silence, the room was growing cold.

"The scriptures say that most of the people who have ever lived went to hell after they died. Because they didn't choose to believe."

"Hell *is* something to think about," he said as a last resort and relaxed his shoulders and smiled. His voice became calm, soothing, talking to a child. "If you're right, then we all go to heaven or wherever after we die. Nothing lost. And even though I was wrong, the only consequence will be that I spent my life believing in something that made me happy, I belonged to a family."

"And if I'm wrong . . ."

"If you're wrong, and I'm right, you know what comes next."

If Jesus were here . . . "Yeah. Except then God would be this hypocrite who tells us to love our enemies, then tortures anyone who insults his ego by not calling him by the right name—deep-fries them for eternity. A tyrant and a monster and a spoiled child. What do we need the devil for, with a God like that?"

"Scott, that's blasphemy."

"Maybe. But if you're right—Doug—there won't be any need to cast me into the lake of fire."

"Watch it. You'd better watch what you say."

I stood up.

"If you're right, I'll fucking jump."

If Jesus were here, he would understand.

When you lose your faith, it echoes.

It is still all the sketch work in your brain, still etched out on cells, still present in the hollowed-out rivulets full of ten-syllabled chemicals that flow between those cells. You think you have run from your faith? Look behind. It followed you through the tabernacle doors. Just stop, just look around, just once. And couldn't you always feel its warm-milk breath on your shoulders? God inside, in shadow, that holy ghost of God? You are haunted by God's ghost.

I sat with God's ghost in classes that had once been happy daily confirmations of a calling.

God called you to be here, and you are here because God has called you. If you were not called, you would not have come.

Catechismal, a child's syntax, a child's logic, carefully cultivated, thoughtfully studied and learned. To be a fundamentalist you must do the dance of circular logic, you must be a lover of paradox. To enter heaven you become a little child.

I clutched my visions, recited gospel-perfect answers, because even old shit is comfortable shit. Trapped and hot and breathless, my visions coughed and sputtered like clogged carburetors, some deep sense of betrayal pushing me ever closer to the brink of standing up and biting out, "Why are we doing this? Have any of you ever really thought about the *consequences* of what we believe?" before security would haul me, kicking and dragging my heels, outside the gates of the campus to be stoned.

I talked with anyone who would listen, bringing conversations to a standstill with questions about the cornerstones of the faith, snide remarks about the Reformation. Sour jokes about the Nicene Creed.

"What a laugh. Political moves. Persecuted men with deep-seated neuroses vying for political power. *That's* church history for you. Wars and blood and robbery, all in the name of a pacifist from Galilee."

"Have you been getting enough sleep lately?"

"Sleep? Sleep? I've been asleep half my *life*."

At night I replayed the looks and arguments, licked my wounds, gorged on desperate pound-cake philosophies that rose and deflated, one after the other, too sticky and too sweet, a long line of half truths and semianswers and numbers and numbers and numbers that came up to nothing. Frustrated, crippled with so close but not enough, so close, so very close, but *we're so very sorry*, and who, after all, *is* this bastard who gives us a little enlightenment?

"Pack up your Bibles, my friends. Run for your lives. It's all coming down, man."

Friends disintegrated, mysteriously, one by one. "Oh, hello, how have you been? Sorry I missed you. Well, gotta run." Chiming in the vocal chords to cover up the bald panic, the healthy sheep tip-toeing away from the dissenter on tiny cloven hooves.

"Did you hear about Scott?"

Their whispers in chapel, hidden and hissing with the turning of gold-leafed paper, hymnal pages.

"No, what?"

"He's lost his salvation."

"No way!"

"Way, man!"

And that was exactly it. That was the way—man. But I was the sinner. We called ourselves saints. I was the sinner, and they were still *saints*. So I lived in fear of the little armchair theologians who used expressions like "Way!"

But now that is over, and I am not afraid.

Maybe just a little afraid.

I went to public meetings where films were shown or special speakers brought in, and I would sit in the front row and raise my hand and stay frozen like that for an hour or more, as everyone else in the room was called on to speak or ask their question, and then the moderator or professor would finally say, "Well, if there are no more questions, we can all go home now."

And they laughed and shook their heads, until I looked back at them.

I walked through them and walked to the speaker, chased him out into the parking lot, if necessary.

"Excuse me . . ."

"Yes, ah, I'm sorry, young man. I'm in a bit of a rush."

"Excuse me, but . . ."

"I really am in a hurry. Alright, briefly, what is it?"

"What if you're wrong?"

I had done my research.

"Do you have any books on apologetics?" I asked the college librarian and frowned.

"A few," she said. "We have a few."

"No, but I mean, books written in argumentation *against* fundamentalism?"

"I'm sorry?"

"You know, books pointing out the fallacies of the church. The gaps in logic. That sort of thing."

She looked at me as if she thought I might be carrying a concealed weapon. Two weeks without shaving and irregular bathing habits probably heightened that effect.

She tried to think the best as she walked me through the stacks.

"Studying up on the enemy?" she asked and smiled.

But I only began pulling out her books, flipping them over like kittens, scanning their backs and their stomachs, shoving them back upside down and out of place. She followed me down the row, rearranging.

"Wrong," I said, but not to her. "No, no, no. This won't do. O God. This is nothing at all."

"Let me know if you need any help," she said and walked away quickly, because I had looked up at that.

The night before midterm exams, and all the preachers-to-be were buried under stacks of books and swallowed white wafers of Vivarin with swigs of Jolt soda. Greek verbs, conjugated, escaped from the cracks under their doors into the hallways, colliding with Hebrew and bumping into the prophets, mingling with memorized patriarchal genealogies, one voice on top of another like musky, scented chanting.

I was in my room, looking for Jesus.

I had deserted the week before, driven to a library that was not connected to a church, a free-standing library with uncensored books. The books stretched out across my desk, my bed, the floor, opened to important pages underlined in pencil markings that I later erased like a good Christian boy.

Rabbis wrote about him. Long writings, critical writings, then the friendlier writings of the Ecumen. Here, in this book, he was a liar. In this one, a lunatic. In that one, in theory, he was a legend. In that pile in the corner, he was still Lord.

But he could be found. It was still too soon to doubt that answers exist. *Knock, and the door will be opened.* Maybe he's hiding out in some kind of mosaic, some clipping together of strings of icons that will finally, in total, mean something. Or maybe he's on the next page.

Knock, knock.

I *knew* that I could find him. In these stacks and notes and dissertations. Or in other books in other libraries. And if I couldn't find him here, I would take a trip to Galilee, get on my knees and dig in the sand until I found a fragment or a potshard or a note written to me, "Dear Scott, it's all true. Quit bitching. Love, God." Love God.

Dig until I found it, found a two-thousand-year-old photograph—or found the goddamned bones and took them back to Calvary.

A knock at the door.

See? It's him.

The figure on the other side of the door was about six three, a Michelangelo block of muscle with coal black hair and crystal blue eyes and naked except for a hand towel wrapped precariously around his waist. A tattoo of a cobra, blue-and-green, wound up from some unseen crevice on his groin and coiled finally around the right pectoral.

"Your name Scott?" he growled through a voice full of gravel.

I nodded, cleared my throat, looked down. Naked men with tattoos were not a common sight on our floor.

"Got a phone call."

"Uh, thanks. Do I know you?"

"Name's Jeff," he said. "Jeff Shepherd." And he shot out a hand with a granite-hard grip.

It's hopscotch and dragonflies and motorbikes the day you go looking for Jeff Shepherd.

It is being new, it is being young again, you need a ten-year-old's imagination and a skip-and-jump heartbeat, comic books and Slurpees, because you are too young to feel guilty.

You brave your classes and you trespass among your old friends to catch him in your peripheral vision, and then you sit, not next to him but near to him, near enough.

"What'd you do over the weekend?" a pretty girl asks him. And he says, "Wrote poetry."

And you like that, you like the way he says that word, Southern and drawled, the way he says it: "po'try," almost "poultry," and you like that.

And you like it that he writes poetry, because the pretty girl does not like it, men in our world cannot write poetry, should not write poetry, may not, must not write poetry.

"No, seriously, what'd you do?"

"Something wrong with your hearing?"

Your heart is in your throat, in your head . . .

"I do some writing too," you say, and then you smile at him, smiling at Jeff Shepherd, and the girl is surrounded.

"Really," he says. Really. Period.

"I'd like to see your work sometime," you say, slithering in through his vanity.

"Really?" And now it's a question. "Yeah, that'd be great. Could be fun."

And he walks away from the table and away from you, bowlegged Southern boy with tattoos no one else here knows about, blue-and-green secret coiled up somewhere on him; he walks away, and in him you see Southern skylines and the lapping of water and the writing of poetry.

When I woke up he was in my room.

There was a sheet that I had draped around my bed to block out the universe and the stares from my non-Buddhist roommates. But just beyond the sheet there was breathing, dark and deep, and the silhouette of someone sitting in my chair reading.

"Shepherd," I said, the way men say each other's names.

"Door was open. Get up."

We drove to a park somewhere in Tequesta, with the windows down and Hank Williams Jr. on the radio.

"God, I need a cigarette," he said.

So I stopped at a store and bought him a pack, one with a camel and a pyramid on the package.

"How'd you know my brand?" he asked. But I couldn't say it had just fit him.

"Jesus was a man," he said, while we sat beside still water and I learned how to smoke. "A real man. A man's man. Not like the stuck-up Christian wimps colleges like ours keep churning out."

I tried on his Ray-Bans.

• • •

He had picked up his nicotine habit in the Navy; then rode with some bikers in north Florida, where he earned his tattoos. He ground his teeth on Southern Baptist religion, but then someone had reconverted him to Jesus and he'd come here to go to school.

He loved a girl who was older, much older. She was divorced and had a child. He wasn't allowed to love that kind of girl.

His poems were mostly about wolves. Good manly poems about lone wolves, and you didn't have to fry any synaptic connections to understand.

"So how do you still believe?" I asked, because the Holy Ghost didn't really fit him.

"Will power," he said.

The goal of our creed and our worship, stated or unstated, was for each of us to become a carbon copy of Jesus, or the generic Jesus painted by the pastors. All grays and cobalt blues and heavy brush strokes. In the end, we looked and dressed and talked and walked like one another; and we called that looking like Jesus.

I loved Jeff because he didn't look like that kind of a Jesus. Not because of his eyes or his hair or his wolves. I loved him because he was as full of color as a stained-glass window in Saint Paul's Cathedral, if then I had ever even heard of Saint Paul's Cathedral. And I was just a clone.

At night we walked along the harbor in West Palm Beach, long past the curfew that was supposed to keep the future shepherds in their own beds, discussing religion, the state of the world, the typical late-teens bullshit. Actually, Jeff discussed these things, stretched them out over his deep-throated drawl, and I listened.

We lay down on the concrete embankment of the inlet, looking out at the Palm Beach skyline and the stars.

We took off our shirts to escape the heat. Jeff moved close enough so that our shoulders touched, barely, the Southern subtext of affection. His skin was smooth, gave off a lazy heat.

"And I don't understand the hang-up about gay guys." He launched into another soliloquy. "I've known a couple. In the Navy. They were just like any other two guys, like best friends. Except they would go home together. Big deal."

"Yeah," I echoed. "Big deal."

"I'll bet some people would think you and I look like we're gay right now," he said.

"Why's that?"

"You know, lying here in the middle of the night. Better hope we don't get attacked by any homophobic joggers."

"Hadn't thought of that. What would you do?"

"I'd look the sons of bitches in the face and say, 'Yeah, I'm a faggot. But I'm still gonna kick your ass. Try explaining that to your girlfriend.' "

Laughter was there, because we thought we were clever. Laughter as clear as water and as open as sky. As basic as the blood in our bodies, warm and alive. It flowed, ran hushed through my heart and mind; like the Holy Ghost, it soothed the soul.

Jesus.

They filled my world with your picture. Sometimes you were angry, sometimes you were gentle, even sweet. No tenderness could be found in God, but *your* eyes—your eyes were the eyes of a lover, as much full of life, as much a part of death. As much between the atoms in our flesh, as stretched out between two stars and crucified.

But your body turned cold when I heard their words. Your body, blue, cold, and stiff. And I thought that the last Christian had died on the cross. The Good Shepherd, a lie or a myth. Another weapon used to beat children. But the children had all grown up, and nobody remembered to tell them that there was no Santa Claus.

But in this night, prayer is a natural thing. And I think for one second that I can see you. You are not hiding, you are not hiding your face from me. And it takes no effort to believe.

You are lying next to me, you are wrapped again in flesh. Sharing warmth and compassion with the body of someone who thinks but still believes.

Christ, touch me.

• • •

So my father phoned and said that he and Joanne were coming to Florida for Christmas vacation. They had Ryan and Joshua with them for the holidays and thought it would be a great idea to load up their Ford Ranger and head to Walt Disney World in Orlando.

Perfect. I could introduce them to Jefferson Shepherd.

I could never introduce them to Jefferson Shepherd.

So I started dating a girl, quickly. Shelly knew I had not been attending services regularly but assumed I had legitimate reasons, so we never talked about my backslidden condition. She was beautiful, the girl every guy in our parish wanted to date, warm and friendly and sexy, someone to introduce to my father. I pictured it, planned it, and hoped in some Freudian way that he would be at least a little bit jealous.

I called him from Shelly's house and left a message on his machine.

"Hi, Dad, looking forward to seeing you! Give me a call tonight, if you get a chance, so we can tie down some plans. I'm at . . . uh, my significant other's house," I said, not wanting to use the word "girlfriend" while Shelly was in the room. Don't push it. Too soon for that. Give it a week.

He called back late, voice scratchy and uncomfortable.

"Well, at least your significant other is a woman," he said.

What the hell was that supposed to mean?

"It looks like we're going to be under some time constraints," he said. "Some things have come up. I don't think we can make it down there."

"Really?"

"I don't suppose you could drive up to Orlando and meet us?"

"No, I could never get the time off from my part-time job."

"Oh. Well, we can see you some other time. No harm done. I'm sure you have lots of friends you can spend Christmas Day with."

"Sure. Lots of friends."

"Well, just wanted to let you know. How are things otherwise?"

"Great, Dad. Everything's great."

The next night I paced back and forth in front of the pay phone in the dorm. No one else asked to use it, because no one talked to me.

Their heads poked out of their doors, they smiled, and they shut their doors again quickly.

I dialed his number, then dialed it again, hung up on the second or third ring. I didn't know what I was going to say. I only knew that there was a dragon curled up and sleeping inside my brain, all hot breath and smoke, restless, stirring.

There were three men in my life.

I pictured him driving to Florida, riding the goddamned rides in Disney World like father of the year.

There were three men in my life, God, Rodney, and my father.

I saw him laughing and talking with Ryan and with Joshua, his *real* sons, the sons from his *real* life, not nightmares from his adolescent hormonal rampage that had crawled out of the grave and now scratched and clawed at his doorstep.

There were three men in my life, God, Rodney, and my father, each of them with turned backs, silhouette.

I saw him making his pretense of affection with my brothers, with my flesh and my blood, and they would never suspect what a cold and distant liar he was, they would never know until they had put their trust and faith in him and he had tossed them aside when parenting became a bore or a struggle, he would toss them aside and begin some other life that was more appealing, more rewarding, he would sigh and grunt and begin again.

There were three men in my life, and two of them had gone away. But one of them, at least, was still within my reach, one of them could be made to pay.

The phone rang the fifth time, and the answering machine clicked to life.

"You have reached the home of Lieutenant Colonel Peck and Captain Schilling. Please leave your message at the sound of the beep." Then a long whine.

And the storm broke.

"Hiya, Dad," throat full of sarcastic ache. "Sorry I missed you. Hope you have fun this vacation with Mickey-fucking-Mouse. By the way, a special Christmas thanks to you for coming into my life and blowing smoke up my ass. Guess all of this New Age relationship bullshit finally got on your nerves, huh? Well, not to worry, because it's all over and done with now. I'm cutting you free. I don't want anything from you, I want nothing to do with you, and there's nothing I want you to do, except of course to go—fuck—your-self."

The machine beeped again and the line went dead. A shame. There was so much more to say. Final words, the closing act. Christ, I would make him pay.

I drive to the drugstore and make it in just as they are closing. The shelves are too neat, far too neat. Boxes lined up in perfect order, too many colors, too much lettering. There are lights in here, long glowing fluorescent lights that make everything look surrealistic, strange. Everything washed out, unfamiliar props in someone else's play.

Yeah, that's it. It must be the lights.

Inside, there is this cloud. Dark and gray and swollen, it has gathered underneath my rib cage and stretched up into my neck and face and brain. My head is stuffed full of something, my eyes think they catch movements around the corners, sudden threatening shivers in shadows that aren't really there.

They disappear when I look in their direction. I have this feeling that anything could disappear, that everything I have been thinking could be made to disappear, if only I could focus on it for a second. Half a second. But the cloud is disorienting; it does not let me focus in, something shrieks out of its center if I even try.

"Can I help you find something," a girl with braces, wrapped up in a white smock, asks.

"No, no thanks. Just browsing. Thanks."

I'm just browsing, that's all. I wander from here to there, I pick up things and look at them, bottles of NyQuil, boxes of cheap stationery.

They sell sleeping pills in economy-sized boxes. Interesting. Vaguely interesting, a fact for someone else.

I carry one of the big boxes to the register, and adrenaline lifts the fog for a millisecond. There is the pounding in my throat. I pick up extraneous items on the way to the counter, where the girl is standing with her glasses on leafing through a magazine.

If she says anything, if she asks anything, I can run.

"Is that all?"

"Yeah. Thanks."

I drive around West Palm for more than an hour, suspicious of every car, every Ford LTD, every Cadillac. I think there is a neon sign above me, an indictment. I wish there were a neon sign above me. The streets are quiet and well lit. Diesel trucks lined up in the lots of Denny's and the Lighthouse Café; teenagers huddle around their cars smoking, and I am driving slowly.

I come to the parking lot of a supermarket in a tiny open-air shopping plaza where a few cars are still scattered and my small Honda can fit in between two of them. I go into hiding and sit there for a long time, notice the wetness in the air, the tight clouds, the conversations of late-night employees walking to their cars.

My car is empty except for me and the big box, opened so I could count the pills one by one and line them up on the car seat. I have a small carton of milk from a drive-through convenience store, and it is opened too. That is all that is in the car, there is no one else with me. God, who was always the given, always the ever-present friend, is not with me. And tonight there are no angels.

I take the pills one by one, slow and deliberate swallows of milk. There are no flashbacks, there are no long internal soliloquies. There is only a kind of quiet, when you surrender to the storm cloud and then it stops being angry and becomes warm and reassuring, drowning you and feeding you in a mother's way.

When the pills are gone I wait, lean back in the car seat, stare up and find the roof of the car, the stains in the upholstery interesting. At first I am tired.

But then my heart begins pounding again. Only this is not from terror, there is no terror in the small person pounding on the inside of my rib cage. It is alien, it is my body knocking, sending out something in Morse code, it is *completely* alien and separate. My mind wants to go to sleep but my body is staying awake, and there is a trembling in the legs, from the groin to the knees. They begin banging against the steering wheel, going numb, and my hands curl up into themselves, like the hands of a quadriplegic. I cannot breathe.

I do not want to die. I never wanted to die. I just wanted to reach into myself and pick out the cells that were hurting. I wanted some skilled surgeon to cut into the soft tissue and target every single cell that carried inside it the memory of something gone wrong.

That cell—a plastic bubble, and inside I see him, I see Rodney with his strap, holding it in the air above my mother's face. Gone. I want that one gone.

That one—there is my father, military regime, unobserved pain and lopsided honor. Get it out. Get rid of it.

Save only the ones that hold bright things. Save only the containers that hold something beautiful, something clean. Let the rest of them go through these death throes, let that other half, that other self, all the cells combined and summed up, let whoever it was who saw and suffered these things go numb and shake, and let his heart pound as if it were exploding, let him die, let him pay.

I step from the car afraid that at any second the ability to move will drain out of me. There is a pay phone against the brick wall of the Winn-Dixie. I reach it and hit the numbers, hitting each one hard, afraid of a loss of concentration.

"Emergency 911," a computerish voice says. "Do you need police, ambulance, or fire department?"

"I, uh, I accidentally took too many sleeping pills, I think."

"How many are we talking about?"

"If you can just tell me what I need to do, that would be great. Should I try to . . . uh, should I try to get rid of them, or . . ."

"How many did you take?"

"A few, I guess. A few too many. A box."

"Can you hold the line for me?"

"I just want to know what to do . . ."

"OK, I'm going to find out for you. Can you hold the line while I look the number up? I'm going to look the number up, and you just stay here on the line while I talk to you, OK?"

"Sure, sure. Thanks."

I didn't notice the police car pull up until the officer was out of his car and walking toward the phone. He took my shoulders firmly, a bored expression on his face, and sat me down on the curb while he took my name.

An ambulance peeled into the parking lot, and people from inside the store came out, staring and talking.

"Took too many sleeping pills?" a handsome paramedic asked as they took me inside the bright white ambulance and began taking my pressure. "Why did we do that?"

"Why did we do that? We don't know. Accident."

"A whole box. That's a hell of an accident. Here, I need you to drink this."

I swallowed a purple vial of some grape-flavored syrup and sat in silence all the way to the hospital, nodding yes or no to their questions. By the time we arrived, I was turning inside out, what seemed like gallons of fluid pouring out of my mouth, with tiny white undigested pills floating on top.

The nurses were flirtatious and friendly.

"Such a nice boy," I heard them saying. "He called me ma'am. Did you hear him? Ma'am."

The doctor, a middle-aged man with a Roman nose and deep eyes, pulled a chair close to my bed.

"Do you think we got all of them?"

"All of what?"

"The pills. You know how many there were. Do you think we got all of them out?"

"I would think so."

"How have you been feeling? Before this?"

"Not so good, I guess. A lot of changes. Just some changes."

"Ah," he said. "Girlfriend trouble."

Sandy appeared about 4 A.M., hair disheveled, makeup smeared and postmodern.

"I'm really sorry about this," I said in the lobby as she walked away from the desk where she had signed a stack of papers. "I know it's late, I'm really sorry . . ."

"I thought you were dead," she said, flatly. "On the phone, I didn't understand them."

"I'm sorry."

Karen stood behind her, her hawkish eyebrows knotted in the middle. I noticed her short-cropped hair, her delicate, handsome physique. So this was who Sandy loved. And Sandy was like a mother. Interesting how the universe shakes us and tosses us into families.

"I thought I'd lost my son."

• • •

Florida no longer fit. The sunshine and the beaches and the casual tanned grace—treasures I had loved and fought to keep—now alien, small, unfriendly.

Days lost their structure. Tuesday nights had always been set apart for volunteer work at the youth group. Wednesday nights filled with Bible study and confession of sins. Sundays belonged to God, morning, noon, and night.

"Do not forsake the gathering of yourselves together." The words of Saint Paul. The church was nothing less than the vine, and we were its branches. It was our lifeline, our mother line, an IV that kept our souls secure and our hearts beating. Without the nourishment of the word, without the communion of the saints, you would starve. Your days are in the hands of God, they move by his calendar.

Now days were just days, just fractions of a week.

Go home, a simple voice said. *Go home. Go and sink your knees into the carpet of the altar again and cry out to God for forgiveness. Ask your brothers for mercy. Tell them you were wrong.*

I circled the church sometimes. Drove around it quickly, hoping no one would notice. Traced an invisible circle, cursed the noose that was too small to ever let me back in.

I spent my days and nights instead with Karen and with Sandy, trying to see them as a couple, eating dinner and watching television at their houses. Poised anxiously on the edge of their sofa, every muscle taut and ready for flight, waiting, moment by moment, for them to start groping each other, making out, tongues lapping at each other's ears, as I would clear my throat and make high-strung excuses to leave.

Instead, we sipped coffee at Karen's dining table and talked about music and art, and there was a space between them, enough room to squeeze in.

I filled that space, listening. Listening for evidence of life.

"I knew I was gay when I was young. Still a kid," Karen said. "You hear it on the playground from first grade on, right? 'Fag.' And nobody wanted to be called a fag. And then you figure out that the name the other kids use when they really want to insult somebody is exactly what you are."

"I can't imagine," I said. "I can't imagine what that must feel like."

"It was different for me," Sandy said. "I loved Bill's father. I loved men. Where I grew up, the word 'lesbian' wasn't used. I didn't know . . . such things were possible."

"So what went wrong?"

"I don't think anything went wrong," she said. "I fell in love with a wonderful woman. One of God's surprises. And we were together for a long time. But she couldn't accept who she was. We never used words like 'lesbian,' not even with each other, not even after eleven years together."

Sandy stared into nothing. The walls, the house, everything was transparent. She looked sideways and backwards through time, until Karen touched her hand.

"We never used words like 'love,' either."

"And then she met me," Karen said. And she could smile like a little girl.

"I wish I had known," Sandy said. "I wish someone had told me that loving someone differently doesn't make you disgusting. It makes you brave."

Words heal. Soak in through your pores. The word sets you free.

Can I tell you something?

Can I tell you that I know what you mean? And that I am beginning to understand what you mean to each other?

Can I tell you about the loves I have hidden and denied, can I tell you about the God I have betrayed—but who must love me anyway to have brought me to this table?

"You look like you have something on your mind," Karen says.

Could I tell you that I love in your way? Can I open my mouth and let the words take shape, can there be a birth here, a new beginning, a discourse? A nativity?

O Jesus, sweet Jesus—my mouth will not open, my lips are dry and my tongue is tight. My spirit, barely stirring after its symbolic baptism. It hurts. There is someone here who is hurting me. Rodney is still somewhere in the hallway, bargaining with the devil and with Honey. They'll tear me up. They'll tear me apart, these three—they'll kill me, if I come out from under the bed.

"Is there something you need to talk about?"

Oh, they'll kill me, if I come out from hiding.

"No, not really." *Can I tell you a secret?* "No. Nothing."

• • •

Honey was scared of microwaves.

She was scared of microwaves and outraged by the things she saw on television every day.

"Kinky sex," she said to me on the phone. "All they want to talk about is kinky sex."

They had moved to Germany after my mother's death, and I had visited them there. I had never known them outside of their house in Maryland, their dark imperial house with its Victorian windows and medieval turret. No child had ever walked up its long path on Halloween, even though we bought candy and waited with it by the door at the end of every October. Children were frightened of that house. Children were frightened inside that house.

They seldom left it. They were so much a part of it, so much its internal organs, that I had caught myself believing they would shimmer and disappear, pop like bubbles, if they ever tried to leave.

But in Germany they had a one-floor flat with high open windows and a brick courtyard full of green meticulously cared-for colors, and the floors were heated by pipes that ran underneath them, so that the house filled with light and heat right up to the German moldings.

And I found it easy, in the little flat, to forgive. And we never talked about my mother. Only once. Once we talked about my mother, and Honey showed me photographs, a little German girl in pigtails and braces. All of my pictures were decapitated.

So when they moved back to Maryland I was sad to hear it. Wondered if they had been allergic to the light. Afraid of all the memories and the life and the little German girls and the light.

They filled their old house with their old furniture and their old paintings and their old presence. Honey called me sometimes to tell me about microwaves and all the kinky sex.

"We so much wanted you to come and live with us after your mother died," she said. And when she was tender she could sound like my mother. "We wanted you to finish high school and then go to college."

"I'm not in school now."

"We would have loved to have had you. We would have paid for everything."

"I'm not going right now. I'd like to, though."

"It's a shame you wouldn't consider coming up here. God gave you to us, you know . . ."

"Yes," I said, "it is a shame."

Sandy wanted me to stay with her.

"Karen loves having you here," she said. "She never had any children."

Too many mothers. Too much family.

"She's really uncomfortable around Bill. I don't think I can ever tell Bill."

"He's your son," I said. "He'll love you."

"I don't know. I don't know that."

I went to the library in Palm Beach. It was tall, and cool inside, and the stacks and shelves of books wound around you, led you downstairs where there were more books, more shelves, more dusty piles.

Jew money had built the place. Isn't that what Rodney had said? Built by Palm Beach Jew money. I thanked God for Jew money. Because these books were forbidden. They were written by unbelievers, scribbled out by the unsaved. Joyce and Nietzsche and Forster and Hemingway. Blasphemers all. They were my brothers, sleeping in between the hard covers of these books, waiting to be read, in a tabernacle built by Jews. They were guides, they had already walked my way, they could lead me into new life.

And the spirits told me I had to go away. I had to go somewhere, someplace where I could read forbidden things without the shadow of the church cutting stripes across my back. I had to go away. I had to go away and learn.

"I'd like to come and live with you," I said, fighting the knot in my stomach.

"That's wonderful!" Honey said. Gamp picked up the phone.

"When can you come?"

"Right away," I said. "Right away."

I spent the final night at Shelly's house. We sat together and talked with her parents, I lied about my reasons for leaving.

"I'm going to the University of Maryland to learn about the unsaved. So I can fight them."

"You'll have to be strong," Shelly's father, who was strong, a good man, said. "You'll have to have faith."

"I have faith."

Late that evening, when it was time to leave, she followed me to my car. I hugged her and whispered into her delicate ear.

"I think I deserve more than that," she said, smiling, and pulled away.

"What's wrong?"

"You've never kissed me."

So she held my shoulders and pressed our lips together. Pain. *This is wrong, this isn't right.* I smiled and blushed and shook her hand.

It would be easy.

It would be easy to put your car into reverse and drive away.

The entrance to their driveway is made of stone, with two tall columns on either side and the rotted remains of a white gate. To the left ahead is the place where my mother fell and we laughed and we planned our escape.

Escape.

But there were lights on inside. Someone, somewhere, was waiting for me to come home.

Inside, the house was warm and its scents familiar. And there was happiness on their faces. My mother could have come into the room at any second, supporting herself on her cane.

Remember your hatred.

But I locked that out. I shoved it out into the cold and focused on their age and on their fragility, on the doors that this could open and on lessons learned about dying. Let her go. Let them go.

They need you. You need them. *Make* this a home.

"We will begin with a discussion of the origins of life," the professor intoned, bored from the top of his bearded head down to his aged tennis shoes. "I know you've all heard this ten thousand times before, so we won't be spending a lot of time on it."

He drew a long thin line on the chalk board, from the left to the right.

"This is time," he said. "History. From the beginning of the world to the present. Does anyone here know how much of this line is taken up with the last ten thousand years?"

Everyone else in the lecture hall raised their hand. The professor walked to the far right of the board and marked off an almost imperceptible fraction of space.

"Right," he said. "You obviously know that it's a space about the width of a fingernail. Makes you feel pretty small, doesn't it?"

Everyone laughed. Almost everyone.

But I could have laughed, laughed at parochial school days that had been a long succession of lectures and sermons held in classrooms attached to church buildings. In biology class, in high school, the first two weeks had been filled with scripture lessons from the book of Genesis.

"The unsaved," our teacher had bellowed, "believe that we evolved from a bunch of monkeys. Christians know that to be a lie. Evolution is only a theory. Scripture is fact."

Later in that same class we learned why it is that whites are more intelligent than blacks. That too was fact.

Now came the collision of fantasy and fact. The class was always restless, other students scribbling notes or pictures or daydreaming. For them this was old hat, boring, easy. But I moved closer and closer to the front row, soaking in every word, staring at the professor so hard that eventually he stared back, talking and gesturing invariably in my direction as if teaching only to me.

"This"—and he drew a huge circle—"is a cell."

If it is so big . . .

"Cells are the building blocks of life."

If it is so big and so terrifying and . . .

"Each cell is a universe unto itself, molecules spinning, and . . ."

Why were they afraid to tell me that it is so big and so wonderful and so terrifying?

They thought you would stop believing. In God. They thought it would make God small.

But if it is all so perfect and sparkling, if there are universes inside a cell—then that is God, and God is truly big.

No one had ever trusted me enough to hand me a set of facts and order me to come to a conclusion. We were given the answers, reality was explained, and all that was required from us was a kind of pious memorization.

Belief is a choice. Try hard to believe.

Here information was tossed out by professors nonchalantly, strings of facts, lists of required reading, make of it what you will—and I loved it that they did not know, nor did they care, about the state of our souls. I trusted them because they did not even know our names.

And I went to sleep at night without saying prayers. Instead I spoke curses to the ones who had presented only one half of every truth and had then threatened children with hell if they dared to question. But the anger was gone by morning, when I could dress and drive to observe my new religion.

You want to write the script.

So here is how it began . . . images fade in on a dark screen, black-border nightmares,

We'll do this in Dolby.

Every boy is an act of creation, every boy is seeing visions. Every boy writing fiction, finding his father in comic books.

In comic books, where the heroes are pigeon-breasted Supermen that you need while you wait for your own chest to swell, while you figure out your muscles and your colors and your veins. You need the men with the iron-cast jawlines, fighting side by side with comrades they would die for gladly, fighting for causes that are plain. Multicolored in their patriotic costumes.

Your father, meanwhile, is in khaki green or navy blue, spread out across the pages in a photo album, little perfect picture squares glued into panels like a comic book.

And what a waste.

Because he was probably like you a long time ago. With his soldiers and his comic books.

I couldn't get comfortable in the Baltimore streets. They crisscrossed and collided and made no sense, out of sequence, no scheme.

So I took I-95, drove with I-95, following it down to Annandale, Virginia, to my father's new address.

He lived in a town house with a brick courtyard in the back and neat shrubs in the front by a sidewalk that was too clean. If you slid your eyes along the rest of their row, other houses, other sidewalks, you could tell when you hit the dividing line—it was their house— with the perfect hedges and the absence of leaves, and you could just tell that it was too clean.

No one came when I pressed their bell, but then you knew that, you knew no one was home.

You are too clean.

I'm living in Maryland.

By what right do you pretend to be clean?

Thought I'd stop by. Sorry I missed you.

You are not clean.

I scribbled a note, left it on their door.

Came back later and retrieved it. Then left it on their door.

Honey answered the phone, and there was a change in her tone, a drop in register, that said it was for me. She dangled the receiver by the cord, and stared out into space.

"It's your father's wife, I think."

"Thank you."

"Current wife."

"Thanks."

Joanne's voice could sweeten anything.

"Got your note," she said, as if nothing had ever been wrong and nothing ever could have been wrong. "Sorry we didn't get to see you."

"I've been busy," I said.

"So have we."

"I've been living with my grandparents."

"I'm sorry." And she laughed. "I'll bet you could use a vacation. Would you like to go on vacation? With us, I mean."

"Maybe."

I got lost on the way to the campsite, lost in the woods in my car, loaded down with baggage and swim gear and an old map my grandfather had given me.

Attendants in tiny broken-wood gas stations pointed to dirt roads and spit and made my buried Southern vowels twang and tumble out of their attic, sharpened by the heat, drowning in handsome Virginia drawls.

When it was dark, or darkening, and I had at least found a road that promised in neon green signs to take me where I was going, I took some deep air and began working on the script.

The script. The one we're all writing.

Because being with him was a battle, a game of chess, and the tension expanded more quickly because no one would acknowledge that we were even playing. Except Joanne. And she hated that we were playing. Cool words and wine, she sabotaged our game.

I practiced my sentences, rehearsed expressions, updated the old routine.

And this, I suppose, is where I should write the epiphany.

If this were a Hollywood Heartbreak Ridge boardroom, the young men with long hair and ties would pull their chairs up to a long glass table and shuffle their notes, fingers, and pencils, tapping, and say, "Alright, boys, let's write the breakthrough scene."

But walking strings of DNA are not privy to our boardroom meetings, and our agents the prophets are all dead or dying, and it was a quiet thing, a simple scene, when I tossed out the script, anyway.

Because he was a boy like me.

With his plastic toy soldiers in the big white house where he grew up with his mother and he wanted to be a marine like his father, who was gone. Like his father, who was sometimes there and mostly gone, or something in between those two extremes.

And he had grown up and gone to *the school*, gone to the academy in Annapolis not far away, ships and sails and boys like him, in white, who wanted to be sailors or marines.

So he wore their whites and became a boy who loved a girl who loved *all* the boys who wanted to be marines.

And one time when they made love, they made a baby. And it was nothing personal, it was no mistake, it was just that when people make love, they often make babies.

And then he went away, and when he came home she was gone, or she was something worse than gone. Just gone to him, and that is worse than gone.

So he let her go. And then the girl had grown up and died, and the baby grew up and wished him dead.

And for which of these sins, I wondered, did I want this boy to be crucified?

The campground was cracked by July, walls of the buildings peeling, the asphalt thick and black and melting. Joanne and her mother hid in the trees playing cribbage; my father and brothers and I stayed in the lake or in the pool, in the water.

Ryan and Joshua fought and climbed up our backs to dive from our shoulders. And my father flirted with teenagers and sucked in his stomach when he jumped in the pool.

Nothing was said. But it was different, it wasn't a sour silence.

"So when you gonna retire, Dad?" I asked.

"I dunno. 'General Peck' has a certain ring to it."

Ryan forgot his towel, shook himself dry by the water, a tiny blond duck.

Nothing else to say.

Ho-mo-sex-u-als.

Get in all the syllables when you say it.

I knew they were around, because I had read they were everywhere. I knew they were on campus, because I had seen the signs. Photocopied, multicolored signs advertising the Gay and Lesbian Organization, GLO, with little lightning bolts or stars around the lettering.

The signs would appear one day and would blow like graffitied, ripped flags the next.

GOD HATES FAGS in black Magic Marker. Or GOD HATES QUERES.

No kidding.

Still, I set out to meet them. And as the new community editor for the university paper, I had the perfect cover.

"I want to cover the campus gay community in the Lifestyle section," I announced to the editor in chief.

"Fine. Sounds good. I'm busy."

"Maybe a whole *series* of articles."

She looked up from her computer screen.

"I don't know. Do you really want to spend that much time around them?"

"Well, it has to be done. It'll be controversial."

"OK, it's your call," she said. "I'm surprised you're doing this. Most guys would feel a little threatened."

"Not me. I know who I am."

They spoke to me as to the enemy.

"The newspapers are full of lies," an angry boy with close-cropped hair railed into my microphone. "It's one big conspiracy."

"So your goal is—what? To let heterosexuals know . . ."

"There are no such things as heterosexuals."

"I'm sorry?"

"Everyone is gay. People like you are stupid and bigots and frauds."

He was right on only one count.

I had interviewed enough of the other "radical" groups on campus to recognize propaganda. It rang in my ears like a migraine headache. Environmentalists on campus, for example, with whom I was extremely sympathetic, tended to look alike and talk alike and bristle at the same questions. It grew old quickly—reel after reel of tape filled up with rehearsed dialogues and brain-deadening interviews. I shelved away the gay students I met as drones of the same variety.

So I was attracted to men. That didn't mean I was one of *them*. Maybe I was some kind of a mutant. I could live with being a mutant. I could not live with being one of *them*.

nine

I loved her. I really did love her. Not one cell in my body could deny that without blushing.

Kelley was a polite hellcat—shyness and sex wrapped up into one beautiful six-foot-tall package with long shock-red hair for ribbons. Beauty was written on her, an objective fact. She sabotaged it, dressed down, floppy fedoras and loose open-front men's shirts—but all of that work just made her riddle more exciting, more inviting, made you want to read it from right to left like Hebrew, made you want to read it with your hands by braille.

And what was that? Was that little-girl reluctance or aggressive expectation teasing from between her teeth, laughing at you in her wet smile?

I met her outside a theater where some bizarre little acting troupe was preparing for a performance. The *Retriever* was covering them, I had already written the article, but our photographer had vanished. So I raced to the show with a thirty-five-millimeter camera and shot frame after frame, kneeling in front of men and women dressed like vampires and hookers and asking them to just act normal.

A fingernail tapped at my right shoulder.

"Hi," she said with a strong voice. "Remember me?"

"No, I'm sorry."

Her eyebrows knotted, a semisecond of frustration.

"I'm Kelley. I'm one of the secretaries at the *Retriever*. You walk past me every day."

"Pleased to meet you."

"Am I that forgettable?"

"No, no . . . definitely not. Uh, how do you know me?"

She smiled a cat's smile.

"I've . . . noticed you."

I watched her after that. Smiled at her on the way into the office, on the way out. She sat at her station like a man, a Camel cigarette cocked to one side of her mouth, her boots propped up on the corner of her desk while she buried herself in Willa Cather, Sylvia Plath.

Without notice, she would change. Transform. Stretch her arms out above her head and arch her back in a lazy feline yawn, then bat her lashes and smile at the nearest man until he stuttered and spilled his words all over himself, shifting his eyes to the floor.

I created work to give her, created urgent messages, any excuse at all to walk to her desk and kneel beside her chair and talk to her about anything.

The men in the office carved her up like a Thanksgiving turkey. We would huddle in tiny circles and discuss her, heterosexual group therapy.

"Nicest piece we've had in here for a looong time," Peter tittered, as if he were *very* clever, *very* astute, really getting away with something.

"I'd like to get me some o' that," someone else said.

"Some of what?" I asked and then laughed quickly, because they were all laughing.

"I mean, a girl like that," Pete said, as if discussing a Matisse. "A girl like that could turn a *fag* straight."

"Damn it!" Kelley howled.

She sat with her legs spread apart, her gigantic satchel open on the floor. She pulled letters, papers, makeup, Kleenex out of the bag and tossed them over her head, letting them fall like dadaist poetry to the floor.

"I can't find my money!" she demanded at me, as if it were somehow my fault.

"I had ten bucks in here this morning! I know I did. I think I did."

"Do you need gas money?" I asked. It was well past closing time, we were the only two left in the office.

"No, no, I'm fine. I live on campus. I'll just starve."

"C'mon, I'll get you some food."

"No, no, no. No sweat. I'll go without. My stomach might bloat and flies might start gathering on my eyelids, and of course I'll be too weak to brush them away, but I'll be fine."

"No, seriously. I'd like to buy you dinner."

She ran a hand through her thick hair and bit her lower lip before she said, "I think I'm in love."

The Pub served cold food and warm beer, but that didn't matter, not that night. She smoked sexually, deep inhales, long, breathy exhales.

"I'm still not used to women smoking," I said, puffing my own Camel.

"How's that?"

"Where I grew up, a guy could get by with smoking. But not a girl."

"Where'd you grow up? Iran?"

"No . . ."

"It's hard to smoke through a veil."

"No, no, I mean, I didn't grow up in the city."

"I didn't either." And she took another drag.

"I wouldn't have guessed that," I said. "Christ, listen to us— whispering like we were recovering addicts or something."

"Born and bred in the Bible Belt," she said, without an accent. Then, reading my face, "I have to be pretty drunk to let it out."

We talked under a gray canopy of smoke, surrounded by music and noise and the smell of nachos and beer. She had run away. Far away from the Bible Belt. Away from Jesus and his people and his belt. And she hid with her accent in this dirty little town that called itself a city.

"So what are you looking for?" I asked.

"Don't know. I haven't got a clue. You tell me. What do you want?"

"A family. Kids. A life. And I'm really blowing it, aren't I?"

"It's not your typical first-date small talk." She smiled, and then stopped smiling. "But then, you don't seem like a typical guy."

And sometimes, a handful of times in one life, you meet someone and feel your spirit click into place. An old and familiar place, and you fit into it with such ease and such sharp grace that you almost hear its *sound*, something like the crack of a dry stick when you step on it in the dark.

"Let me make you a drink," she said.

Our friend's apartment was choked up with people, college students. We began the evening with an attempt at professionalism. We were journalists—we were supposed to sit about and discuss politics, act intelligent.

Then someone showed up with an obscene amount of liquor, and the stereo grew louder by degrees, the conversations more absurd, and Kelley's little drinks harsher until they curled my tongue like rubbing alcohol and scattered rainbows around the ceiling lamp.

"Oh, I'm sorry," she cooed. "The guys I know from Delta Chi drink this like water. Let me get you some *milk*."

"Give me that," I said, and drained it in one long gulp.

I watched with detached disinterest as campus security appeared at the door two or three times, threatening. Kelley sat down on my lap. Amazing, the softness. The lightweight, brittle little bird's bones she must have. The music would fade and then climb up again until it looked as if the bass beats were shaking loose the refrigerator door.

Then she turned, and her mouth was open on mine, warm tongue filling and intrusive and damp.

The invasion was sobering, I wanted to get up, wanted to be alone. But an entire room full of people was watching, pretending not to watch. What would a man do in a situation like this?

I didn't know. She stood up and took my hand.

"Scott and I are taking a tour of your apartment," she said to our host, who responded with a fake scowl of disapproval.

"You two be good," she said, wagging a maternal finger at us.

In a back hallway she pushed me against the wall with masculine aggression. Alcohol gave my hands permission to search her body. I searched, sliding and massaging, groping for a hidden key, listening for any response in my waist, praying for any trembling or excitement, any voice giving direction.

When there is nothing, I take her by her waist and guide her gently onto the floor, ease myself into the groove between her thighs, and begin moving back and forth, our clothes sliding against each other, sparking in the cold dark. I stretch out against her while our mouths are in combat. I feel her tongue in my mouth, circling, darting from one side to the other. There is tremendous heat here, tremendous friction between us—there is everything here, everything you could desire. Except desire. *Christ, you little faggot, I hate you*, keep pushing, keep waiting.

The hallway door opens, flooding us with light.

"Oh, Jesus, I'm sorry," a voice says, and the door slams shut again.

I look down at her.

"So I guess this means you like me," I said.

"No," she answered seriously, "but I could get used to you."

And I kissed her when she smiled.

If there was ever a woman with hands small enough, eyes kind enough, or spirit filled with enough subdued violence to turn a gay man straight, I suppose that I have knelt by her and talked to her and shared my life with her for a little while.

But there is never enough, not even enough love, to reach inside another body and pull at unseen strings, rearrange preordained nerves and cells and chemistry, reorder the course of blood or DNA until someone's way of loving turns in upon itself and becomes something altogether different, new. There is never enough to smear God's grand design and call into being what was never meant to be.

Never. No matter . . . never.

· · ·

So I met Mike in this sunny square we called the Quad.

He lounged by a stone wall, one arm wrapped around the neck of a guitar, his intense dark eyes sucking up the words on the page of the book in his hands.

"You're in Greek 202, aren't you?" I asked.

"Yeah," he said, looking up. "So are you."

He was exactly good looking. He had short blond hair cut close in Navy style. His bones were small, muscles tight like copper wire.

"Do we have an exam today?" I asked.

"Sure do."

"Shit."

"I take it you didn't study?"

"No, I was out late. With my girlfriend."

"You work for the paper, don't you?" he asked. "Didn't you write that article—the one about the gays?"

"Yeah, I did."

"I liked it. Who's your girlfriend?"

"Kelley." And I gave her last name.

"Noooo shit. Way to go."

"Yeah, thanks, whatever. Do you mind if I take a look at your notes?"

And that was it. That was the start.

He played the guitar and I still played the piano, so we commandeered practice rooms in the music department and worked on numbers. We thought we might play New Age jazz in the university pub. Kelley came to our sessions, sat on the floor, and watched me while I played. Mike watched Kelley.

"You guys don't mind my being here, do you?" she asked.

"Not a bit," Mike gleamed. "You give me inspiration."

"How about you, Scott?"

"No, of course not. C'mon, man, we've got a lot of work to do."

"Don't you think Kelley's inspiring?"

"Huh? Yeah, yeah, of course. What about this progression?"

"I think she is," he said, touching her arm. "A regular muse."

Kelley shifted out of his reach.

Mike slouched on the sofa and strummed his guitar, random chords. CNN was on, the sound low. We talked over the notes and the announcers, topics shifting, our thoughts half present.

"Hey, how's your friend?" I asked. "What the hell's his name? John? Jim?"

"John."

"Yeah, John. Haven't seen him around."

"He's been acting weird," he said. "Ever since I started hanging out with you guys. With you and Kelley. If I didn't know better, I'd think he was jealous."

"Maybe he's a fag," I said, shrugging. "They cling to straight guys like a virus, y'know?"

"Yeah," he said. "Yeah, I hadn't thought of that." We paused to watch a frenetic commercial.

"Hey, have you ever thought about that?" he said.

"About what?"

"You know, doing it with a guy. They say every guy's got a few ho-mo-sex-u-al fantasies."

"Hadn't noticed any."

Silence.

"Well, just between you and me," he said, "I've always wondered. What it would be like, y'know?"

"No shit."

"Does that freak you out?"

"Nah," I said. "Just don't get any ideas about me."

We laughed.

Mike was at the party.

I sat near him, swigging a Coors, ignoring a circle of friends. Kelley was late.

His presence made me bristle and I wanted him to leave, wanted him to take his goddamned guitar and go home. I wanted him gone, and I didn't want to think about the *why* of it, about why every word out of his mouth was an irritation.

"Where are you going, bud?" he asked when I stood and walked out toward the balcony.

"Just outside to wait for Kelley."

He followed, and we stood three feet apart in the cold.

"Something's wrong," he said.

I tried to say something, but sentences became growls or frustrated exhales.

"Whatever it is," he said, "you can tell me, man. I won't be offended by anything you say. Or is it about Kelley?"

"I haven't fucked Kelley."

"OK," he said uncertainly. "I'll bite. Why not?"

"I dunno. I haven't. Don't get me wrong—I *want* to. It's just that . . . I might want to try it with a guy, you know? Just once. First, I think. See what it's like."

He shrugged.

"So? I could go for that, too."

"Yeah, I know."

"I've been thinking a lot about it lately," he said, and I looked around his face for shame, for embarrassment.

Nothing.

"Yeah, yeah, I know," I said. "I could tell. And I remember what you said."

"You got a cigarette?" I put it in his mouth, lit it.

"I've thought it all out," I said, watching my hand shake while I lit a smoke of my own. "You and I are friends, right?"

"Sure. Right."

"And I know you're not a fag, so it's not like we'd fall in love or anything."

"Right."

"No love poems. No flowers."

"Yeah, I see. I get your drift."

"It'd just be to try it, y'know? Just to do it. Just to say we'd done it."

He raised his eyebrows.

"Well, not to say we'd done it. You know what I mean. No one would ever know the difference."

He nodded, looked around, and leaned into me like a conspirator.

"I'm getting a hard on right now," he said, "just thinking about it."

I looked up from the balcony and saw Kelley. She saw and lifted up her hand, smiling porcelain.

Judas.

"Let's get out of here," I said. "Let's fucking get this over with."

I passed Kelley at the bottom of the stairs leading up to the apartment.

"Where are you going?" she asked.

"Just over to Mike's."

"Oh, alright. When are you coming back?"

"Not tonight."

"Well . . . then what the hell am I doing here?"

"I'm sorry. I've got to go. I've just got some things on my mind, that's all."

"Fine," she said. "Whatever."

I started to walk away.

"No good-bye kiss, either?"

I walked back ashamed and kissed her lightly on the cheek.

"Gee, thanks," she said, turning and climbing the stairs. "Oh, the passion. Stop, stop."

Inside Mike's apartment, I wrapped my arms around him and felt his pulse pounding loud and fast in the veins of his neck. We started back toward his room, but then he wanted a drink, so we went into the kitchen.

He poured whiskey and started talking about things, anything, everything, nervously and too quickly. He talked about Kelley, about how I felt about her, he asked if I loved her.

"I don't know."

I love you.

"Oh. You should, you know. You will. She's a great girl."

"I know. The best. It's getting late. Why don't we, uh, you know."

"Yeah. Hey, about that other thing," he said. "What we were talking about on the balcony."

"Uh-huh."

"Jesus, was I drunk!" he said, laughing, touching my shoulder. "We were pretty drunk, weren't we?"

"Yeah," I lied. "Yeah, I guess we were."

"I mean, I might want to do something like that someday, but . . ."

"Yeah, me too. No problem. Jesus, we were drunk."

He didn't love me, and he talked too much about Kelley. I talked about her too, but when he talked, he looked hungry.

Late, in his room, we drank whiskey. I could predict his expressions and his way and his mood, down to the muscles in his throat when he swallowed. It made me thirsty.

"I've got to tell you something," he said.

And I knew, I knew, I knew.

"I think I'm in love with Kelley," he said. "I think I'm hot for your girlfriend."

"Really."

"I'm sorry."

"I'm sorry too."

The end of the year approached, and Joanne called from Virginia.

"We're having a New Year's party," she said. "We'd like you to come down."

"Alright," I said. "Can I bring a date?"

Kelley was nervous about meeting my father, but she said yes.

"No offense, Scott," she said, "but it'll be nice not having Mike around."

"You don't like him?"

"He's alright. But we never have any time alone. Just you and me."

"Good," I said. "I don't like him."

It was another day when I took her to my father's house. The last day of December, with dry-twig, burning-leaf wind that wrapped you up in black jackets and overcoats and dusted your windshield with ice and bark. A day that shoves at you, the cold corpse of another year, and you think dead thoughts about yourself and build little fires and drink warm wine and wait for the something that happens at midnight. That some new thing you wait for every year, and you drink so much because it never comes.

Just a day, the last day of the year, the last day.

Kelley spent the Christmas break with her mother in Delaware. I made the drive, made plans.

Her mother met me at the door, a handsome woman, nineteenth-century strength, thick brown hair cut sharply up and away from her jawline and her face.

I'm here to have sex with your daughter.

"Hello," I said and crinkled the corners of my eyes for the all-American smile. "I'm Scott. Pleased to meet you."

"Come in. Kelley's almost ready."

Your home is neat. I require neatness, I like order. That is why I'm here. To bring order. And I'm here to have sex with your daughter.

Kelley ran down the thin hallway in her black heels, tugging at elaborate coils of hair, smiling and talking and dropping an earring. She was in black from just below her collarbone and shoulders to just above her knees, and I loved her completely, if not physically. Ethereally.

That's bullshit.

"You look beautiful," her mother said.

"Beautiful," I repeated. And more beautiful for knowing you are beautiful.

You are here. You are here for me. If you exist, you exist to have sex with me.

The Cure moved around my father's living room in a swell of middle-aged marines who circled her and talked too long and smiled too much like boys and pissed off their wives, who sat on stools in the kitchen and talked to Joanne and to me.

"She's wonderful," Joanne whispered while she poured more wine. "Remember, it's up to you to make me a grandmother."

"I'm trying," I lied, and we both laughed, because it was a good lie.

• • •

I drank enough wine to follow her into her crowd of fans and watched, numbly, her smiling and the turns of her head and her blushing.

And this is the part where the man feels jealousy; yes, that is clearly in the script, this is the part where the man is threatened and jealous. But she is too beautiful for that, and she is smiling. I tried to be jealous of the Cure, *they* don't need the Cure, they don't have the disease. But the flush of her skin, her embarrassment . . . for a semisecond, I am human.

At midnight we sang.

"We've told the boys not to go down into the basement tomorrow morning," Joanne said when the party was over and the final guests had stumbled home. "There's a guest bedroom and a den with a sofa."

"Ahh, I see," I said, relieved.

"You two can work out sleeping arrangements however you would like."

I started drinking heavily.

Joanne and my father walked upstairs together at last, flirting, my father winking and smiling. And I had waited twenty-one years for that carnivore's smile, those teeth, that man-to-man and man-oh-man smile.

I stayed in the living room and poured more wine, searched for the vodka impatiently.

The Cure stumbled, and we laughed.

"Drunkard," I whispered.

"Oh, fuck you," she whispered back and smiled a Cheshire smile and then took off her heels. I took her waist and kneaded it and pulled until her hipbones thumped sharply against mine, and kissed her, half drunk.

"Don't wake up my parents." Half hoping someone would hear and think. Think.

Think about it.
"How about a cigarette?" I asked her.

We crept out into the back courtyard, red brick and frozen plants and the steamy hum of an outdoor ventilator.

She rocked back and forth on bare feet and puffed angrily, impatiently, while I stood still and breathed.

"Who else has there been?" I asked. "Who was there before me?"

She gave a name.

"What happened?"

"I don't know. I didn't know. Why are we talking about this?"

"I want to know."

"We went out a few months. We were very intimate, you know what I mean."

"Yes."

"Or maybe you don't, church boy."

"I know what you mean."

"It's freezing out here," she said, took a deep drag on her cigarette, waited. "Anyway, one day it just stopped. Everything. He didn't return my calls, he wouldn't talk to me, nothing. Turns out he was gay."

"No kidding."

"No kidding." And she was shaking, throat tightening. "I know I shouldn't feel angry. It's just, I'd had so much hope, you know? He just walked, no explanation, no 'I'm sorry,' no nothing. Next thing I know he's telling everyone that he's gay."

"Son of a bitch," I said. "That son of a bitch."

She looked through me when I lit a second smoke.

"Don't you want to know?"

"Know what?" she asked, shivering.

"Who else . . ."

"I know," she said. "I know. You think I'll be your first. I know."

"How?"

"Just know."

"I want you . . . in my bed tonight."

"I know."

• • •

Somewhere in the tangle of bodies and passion and heat, God will shout out light, constellations will scatter. I will want her in the way that men want women, everything turned inside out—and after this night, even the thought of making love with a man will sound surreal. Hallelujah, it is written.

Memories, dreams, wasted prayers, all fade tonight, prepare for the ascent of the Christ, all pass through judgment on this the last day, and two will become one in a room beneath my father's bed, in my father's house, full circle, like the sun and the moon and the stars and the year.

Stop. Stop it.

Oh, wait. Wait for the tenderness.

We will marry. Soon. And have children. Two. And we will both have to work at first, but in time I will graduate and find a job at a newspaper, and we should have my parents over for dinner, and they should lean over our baby's crib and coo and say, "She looks just like Kelley," sweet little pink little proof of the cure.

And my father should smile in a melancholy way and say, "She looks like your mother," and with the word bring everything around in full, cementing all gaps, granting asylum and a conclusion and a meaning to history, firing the future in solid, hard steel, everything final and everything pure.

"I don't know . . . I don't know exactly what to do."

"Let me explain." And she lifted off my shirt, skirting it around my shoulders. "It goes something like this . . ."

And maybe someday I would have a son and he would come to me and ask about homosexuality. And maybe he would have a worried look on his face. And I would smile at him firmly and knowingly and say, "Son, every man experiences these feelings," smooth baritone voice, "but don't you worry. You'll grow out of this the way you grew out of your shoes. Just put it out of your mind. Here, here's five bucks. Why don't you take a nice girl to a movie?"

. . .

Stripped naked, I lay Kelley across the bed, sliding up on top of her, hoping she would not notice the physical evidence, my body's betrayal.

I buried my face into her belly, kissing her beautiful skin, appreciating it, but with distance, with love projected on a screen, unreal, detached. I kissed her breasts slowly and curiously, loving her response and her hands in my hair.

Loving everything but this, I don't want this, every little nerve ending retracting, I don't want this, *Jesus!*

War, war, fight it.

I have told you the way it should be, but my body and this fucking bedroom with no windows are saying something, or Someone somewhere has spoken . . .

I slide my hand between my legs and try to force something, anything, but it is more than the groin, it is more than that, it is something inside and everything inside, it *is* war, it is *mutiny,* it is no future and no babies, no sense and no conclusion, it is no circles or cycles, and no man-to-man talks about little girls with little boys who were never meant to be.

She moves me onto my back, and her hair trails down across my chest and then abdomen.

Nothing.

And then warmth and moisture.

Nothing.

Oh, Christ, Christ, I can't believe this is happening.

"Don't worry," she says. "It happens."

But there is a vague insult in her words, I know it. I can feel it. If nothing else, I am still a man, with a man's pride.

Ha.

A lifetime cultivating masculinity, trying at least to be a man. And now, where is this creation, this man, this Adam? Withered. Disgusted and disgusting. Beaten down in my father's house, deflating the cycle, whipped and beaten.

Even though I had done everything the way I was supposed to do it, even though it had cost me more. What other man had ever had to make a discipline out of this sort of thing, what other man had had to practice desire or had prayed so hard to gain what should be his birthright?

If I close my eyes and think of men, there is something. If I thicken her voice and her skin in my mind, there is something.

But that is nothing.

I move Kelley onto her back, hoping she will forget my failure. I *will* make her feel satisfied, I *will* prove to her that I am capable of satisfying, I am capable, I am satisfying a woman. I *will* prove to her that I am not like that other, I am no faggot. I *will* prove I am a man.

Lift her leg by the ankle, kiss the thigh, zero into the heat, move your face closer and closer to her heat.

And I baptize myself in her body.

We lay down together finally to sleep. Kelley moved to touch me, but I turned away softly and pretended to fall asleep. When I thought she had drifted off, I crept out of bed, found my pants, and walked into the hallway bathroom.

My stomach was churning, muscles collapsing, I made it into the Southwestern bathroom and vomited. When a heterosexual man has sex with other men, in prison maybe, maybe to stay alive, maybe because that was what he was expected to do—was this it? Was this what he felt?

Kelley became real, filled out into all three dimensions in the next room, and I loved her because I had hurt her, the family tradition. Love twisted and tangled and brutal and needy and bleeding, and still love.

I love you.

That is what I should say. I could mean it. I do. I love you.

In the wrong way. As if you were another bruise on my family.

And I spilled my stomach again and again and again, since I had just made love to my sister.

• • •

"What's wrong?" she asked again. "I blew it, didn't I?"

There had been mostly silence on the road to Delaware.

"No, of course not."

"I did. I blew it," she said resignedly. "I knew I had too much to drink. Your parents noticed, didn't they?"

"No . . ."

"What am I saying, did they notice? How couldn't they notice? I was careening into walls, for Christ's sake."

"They didn't notice. They said you were wonderful. They liked you."

"No, come on, you can tell me, really. Oh, God, what did they say? Jesus, I know I blew it."

She didn't cry, out of spite.

And you wanted to say more, you little faggot, you wanted to explain, but the words were dry and sticky water in your throat.

I was Franz Kafka in the backseat of Mike's car. Stretched out and hiding while he smoked his joint and watched for the "fascists," the campus police. He smoked his joint, and I was this little roach in hiding. On my back, dying.

He took a long drag and let it creep out of his mouth, a gray dragon.

"I slept with Kelley," he said.

"My Kelley?"

"Yeah."

"When?" I asked, interested only distantly, as if asking about the weather.

"Thursday. Last week."

It was someone else who kicked at the seat, missed the back of his head.

"What's wrong?" he yelled. "You couldn't do it. What's wrong with you?"

"Let me out of this goddamned car!"

"Alright, alright," he said, reaching across and opening the door, dropping his joint.

"I just wanted to make things right," he said, while he fumbled on the floorboard for the butt. "I just wanted this to be over."

"It's over," I said. "You can bet your sweet ass it's over. I hope you two will be real fucking happy with each other."

I started running, heat pumping fast into my face and ears, oblivious to the subzero weather. I found a pay phone and called her. "Is there anything you want to tell me?"

"What do you mean?"

"Is there anything you have to say? Any little piece of trivia I should be made aware of?"

"Oh, God, Scott, let me explain . . ."

"There's nothing to explain. One word. A yes or a no, that's all. You fucked him?"

"Yes."

"Then fuck you."

"I don't love him," she said when we saw each other again.

"I do," I said, even though that was a lie.

There was nothing, not even surprise. She just looked tired. We lit fresh cigarettes when Mike came in.

Kelley sat with her back against the wall and spared nothing, missed nothing, the muscles in her face working conspiratorially with the bones and the eyes to *create* a face, a beacon. Her arms and her hair and her body, all words and all language—she shot out femininity and sex in all directions, with distraction, indiscriminating, striking out and then pulling back until the eyes and attention of men and women found her, riveted on her, blood and heat and motion.

"Everyone's looking at you," I said, jealous and weak.

"Really?" And then a cutthroat smile.

And I sat stiffly, proud and puffed up like a son of God, with warm draft beer and a Camel cigarette that I bit between my teeth to look more like a man, like someone rugged and reared and prepared and assured, assured, assured that he was a son of God. One of the elect, the chosen few. Proud. Puffed up like another of God's old wounds.

"Well, we really fucked things up, didn't we?" Mike sat still and stared at the table top curiously, human, missing something.

"Don't blame your*self*, Mike," she said and touched him, absently, not absently. With precise vengeance. And in his shoulders there was a subtle flinch.

When he left for drinks, she leaned forward, whispered: "Did you really say those things?"

"What?"

And she listed them. Whore, useless, baggage, whore.

And his other words, biased assurances: "Scott will never love you. Scott will never be with you. Scott will never make love to you."

"Did you say those things?"

"Never."

She leaned back and calculated.

"That's what he said." And she was white. "That's how he got me."

I am quick when he comes back. Quick and clever and belittling, and I diminish him. Anyone listening would know that I diminish him for her, for some sick Christian sense of chivalry. But he does not notice, he only registers her, he knows I cannot touch him.

He has immunity. A gift of God for a son of God. Genetic immunity, safe from rough skin, from men's eyes, from thick torsos and legs and tight-muscled waists. I am only wasted, like her. With her skill, I could drag him out and make him beg, make him bleed, make him love me, and then laugh at him and hand him a rope outside the gates of the city.

But he was in some other world—impossible, juxtaposed and inverted. Cutting Mike was a business for Kelley; she could not touch me. She did not think she could touch me. And Mike could only cut me, which he had already done and done so well, and there were other things now that required his attention. And only I could cut Kelley, which would have been redundant. And so we sat together quietly, wasted with all our outrage.

t e n

Honey knocked on my door at night. Not out of meanness—maybe meanness, maybe at first. Later it was just routine.

The end of the world was coming. Her spiritual guide, some slow-voiced guru on the radio, had told her the final storm was fast approaching and only the elect would survive.

"You're in sin," she said and sounded bored after the first few weeks.

"How do you know?"

"You're in sin. You're in terrible, terrible sin."

And "sin" conjures up nothing in me except brilliant, sparkling pictures of cancer and diseases and pale skin.

So I combed over my body in the shower while the water was hot. Hot enough to make you dizzy and lose your breath. Took my skin and divided it up mentally into blocks, into surveyor's lots, looking for something, anything. Signs of sexual disease, even though I had never made love and no one had ever made love to me. Blue patches of rough skin or freckles that I convinced myself were growing. I waited for the wages of God, the malignant incarnation of sin.

She left articles on my door, roughly taped, that I found when I came home from work or from school, clippings from magazines and newsletters from ministries, from Jerry Falwell. *Sodomy and Special Rights. The Gay Conspiracy. Gays Want Your Children. Thank God for AIDS.*

"You've probably become homosexual," she said, sighing and resigned. "They're all homosexuals at colleges these days. And I found your pictures. The pictures of boys."

"They're not boys."

"Movie stars, whoever they are. You're too old to have crushes on movie stars."

So I found a picture of Cindy Crawford naked in a magazine, arms covering her chest, legs crossed conveniently. I clipped it and taped it to my wall. But by then I was tired and just wanted to leave.

It was hard to find a roommate, because I told them I might become bisexual.

"I'm not saying it's going to happen," I said to one and then another and then another. "But it might. It could happen."

And they would say it was alright, because they knew me and liked me. They laughed it off, said I was just cracking up. Said the right woman could fix me, said I should get back together with Kelley.

"That bullshit with Mike could make any guy think he was a fag."

"Maybe," I said. "No, actually, it's always been that way."

"So you're gay?"

"No, God no. No, it's just a theory. A political thing, in a way. I can go either way."

"Have you?"

"No, but I could. I might. I just want you to know."

And then they would back up a pace, or their heads would lean back a little into their necks, their shoulder blades, as though this explosion might suddenly take place, might shower them with chiffon and turn them into screaming faggots.

Screaming faggots.

I combed the campus looking for gays. Looking for men who were not screaming faggots.

I knew where the campus gay and lesbian group met and what time to be there. I called ahead, feigned interest in writing another story, made sure the meeting would be held on schedule.

The room was clean and white and big, with twenty or more

chairs set up in a semicircle that fanned out to the walls. I arrived a few minutes late to avoid any questions or welcomes.

I sat uncomfortably, quietly, a few seats back from the front, with an entire row to myself. The faces were tight and tense and slightly petrified, except for a girl in the front row who spoke constantly, slurring her words around a submarine sandwich.

"We need to reconsider our name," she said.

"Not this again," a boy with a Christmas bulb hanging from his right ear moaned.

"Why does the word 'gay' appear before the word 'lesbian' in our club name? And what about bisexuals? There's no mention of bisexuals whatsoever."

" 'GLO' is a catchy name," said a male mouse. "What would we call it if we put 'lesbian' first?"

"It's misogynistic," *chomp, chomp, chomp, gulp.*

Something about her food was mesmerizing. The muscles around her jawline worked, circled, and her off-color tongue lapped out shamelessly at mayonnaise on her cheek. The boys squeaked their comments or questions, embarrassed objections. But she lapped them all up, clipped out wet responses. They waited, coughed, paused, looked around. Her chewing and swallowing covered all silences.

"By the way," the boy I assumed was the president said at last, "we may need to file a complaint." Speaking made him nervous, made him shake so that his earrings dangled against his cheeks.

"Against who?" *chomp, chomp.*

"Did anyone else hear those guys outside when we were walking in? They said 'fag' under their breath."

Outrage.

"Did you bash 'em back? Did you bash 'em back?" She practically dropped the hoagie in fury, lifting one hand and shaking it menacingly.

"We gotta get in their faces and *bash!* Tell 'em, I'm not a fag, I'm *queer! Queer!* I take it up the ass and I love it!"

I tried to imagine that, tried to imagine walking up to a guy and telling him I was queer, telling him something about my sex life or lack thereof.

Tried to imagine him being the enemy, while they talked about the enemy.

The enemy: the white heterosexual male. Guilty of blood, guilty of everything from drugs to crime to poverty to misogyny to the hole in the ozone layer. Guilty en masse and guilty in theory, the suburban scapegoat. And I believed them for a second, because I always want to believe in your theories.

Until I hold faces up to your theories.

I moved in with Russell because he said he didn't give a shit who I slept with, because he knew he was straight.

We sat on my grandparents' porch, and when floorboards creaked above our heads, I would stop talking and hold up my hand to silence him, and we swatted at invisible bugs, waited.

"I've heard some guys try this out," he said. "Usually right before they get married."

"Do you have any idea how betrayed we feel?" Honey asked the final day, while I dragged cardboard boxes around her.

"Betrayed?"

"You're not exactly the person we raised you to be. You're not what we wanted for a grandson."

"I'm good to people. I'm honest. I care about you."

"You're unsaved."

And then she smiled, but it was not the smile that made her look like my mother.

I have seen the boys on Eager Street beside the bars with blackened windows and mirrored doors. And red-brick alleyways where they loiter after closing. Smoking cigarettes and stroking their manes, posing and playacting and looking strong.

Then, it was only another street, crowded with young lions in leather jackets and summer tans, intimidating for reasons I could not have explained, intimidating from my car, and once or twice I circled the block while my heart thudded dully and I avoided their eyes.

• • •

That summer I was rich, or thought I was rich, with a summer job in a condominium near the harbor. The environment was rich, elite, a garden and an indoor pool. I could sit at a desk from afternoon until late at night reading, glancing now and then at a video screen to make sure no one was creeping onto the property. Everyone was safe.

I was not safe driving to work, crossing over Eager Street, breaking an invisible boundary line and risking everything. Truth, always so fucking threatening. I would rather they had been carrying crowbars and switchblades. But afterward I could sit behind bullet-proof glass and greet the residents when they came or left, push a button to let them in, smiling, making them feel safe. Everyone is safe, until the drive home again.

The residents were mostly men, single or with roommates. Some were artists and musicians, my age, with chic jobs and sports cars; others were older—executives or architects. I had not been trained to make the connections. I came to recognize them by their smiles or by the rhythm of their days.

There was Bill, a handsome forty-something black man with James Earl Jones's voice and a quarterback's handsome thickness. He came home at five, pressed suit and tie, rich patent leather briefcase. Then by six sounds leaked out from under his doorway, music, and his baritone voice rumbled out into the hallway, rolling waves of Verdi or sometimes German, drunk on Wagner.

Some days were louder than others, and residents came to me to complain. I would promise to knock on his door, make him stop; and then I waited with eyes closed for him to finish, feeling his bass shake the bullet-proof barrier.

I was perpetually embarrassed for Paul, the architect with short bleached-blond hair, who redecorated his apartment every two or three weeks. Teams of movers with rough hands and bright neon orange trolleys swarmed past my desk while Paul hovered and fretted around them.

"That's a Remington," he would say, as if speaking to very slow children. "Rem-ing-ton. More expensive than a black-market kidney. Worth more to me than your lives. All of your lives. Get it?"

I looked up from my desk one day to see a bust of a naked woman with a terrified expression on her face. Paul's well-groomed head poked around from behind her.

"What do you think?" he asked, obviously deeply concerned. "Honestly. I'm looking for gut-level reactions here."

"I think, uh . . ."

"Too farcical, right?"

"I don't know, maybe . . ."

"Too Andy-Warhol-takes-on-neoclassicism?"

"Yeah, sure. Whatever."

"I knew it," he moaned, banging his head on the statue. "The LSD's kicking in again. My bedroom looks like the best little whorehouse in Baltimore. Oh, God. All I need now are red velvet drapes."

Red velvet drapes. Everything I knew about gay men could be summed up and surrounded and covered with red velvet drapes.

Everyone knew. And if you had to, you could say it in a single-syllabled word: *weak*. Gay men wanted, really, to be women. Instead they became painted, pathetic parodies of the female of our species, the *weaker* sex. There were no exceptions. Every limp-wristed one of them was the same. Every faggot was a coward, every hairdresser a traitor to the race.

Coincidentally, I was one of them.

What stared back when I looked in the mirror was some kind of illusion, some temporary disguise. In time, though, I was resigned to the sickness becoming apparent. One day I would awaken to find myself intensely interested in French poodles and interior decorating. I would go to the opera and cry—and then lisp excitedly to my boyfriends about what a great evening I had had. And then we would all go to a Motel Six and have group sex, being cautious all the while not to mess up our hair.

I didn't know how it would happen or when. But the collective wimpdom of homosexuals was an empirical fact. And in time the gay storm troopers would come to disconnect the muscles controlling my wrists.

After that I would slash them.

When John Ryder walked by, I could have choked on the shame.

His walk inspired shame. The strength in the shoulders, the rippling and flexing muscles around his waist, the ice-water eyes. It was all disgrace and all shame.

He came home every day at the same time, disappeared behind closing elevator doors, and then reappeared exactly fifteen minutes later, dressed in tank tops or sweatshirts, on his way to the gym. Two hours later to the minute he returned, with a white towel draped around his neck and his hair darker and wet with sweat.

"Are you a student?" he asked one day. And the vowels betrayed him: New York, tough and flippant, masculine and alien.

"Yeah, I am. How did you know?"

"You don't look like the type who would read Baudelaire unless some sadist was forcing him to."

"Thanks. I guess. Going to the gym?"

"Yeah." And he opened the glass door with his back. "Look, if you ever get bored down here, let me know. I've got some great stuff you could stand to read."

"OK."

"Great. I'll drop them by. Most of them are in translation. I don't suppose you can read Greek?"

"No, not well."

"Well, we'll work on that too."

He hurried by in the mornings, slowing just long enough to slide Thucydides across my desk.

"There'll be a quiz when I get home."

And Lucretius, Aristotle, and Aeschylus, and finally Plato's *Phaedrus*.

"This is my favorite." And he bared his perfect teeth.

Phaedrus. Just words, just conversations. Words between men about men, about men who loved men without becoming women. And I made them into warriors instead of philosophers, stone-white statues come to life long enough to laugh and joke on Athenian roads, strap their arms around each other's necks and then make love in tall grass. Make love roughly.

And those statues were another reason, on a long list, for being deeply ashamed. Because that was not why John Ryder had brought these books to me, these were not the images I was supposed to see. He brought the books because I was a man and he was a man; and no one knew men or men's souls better than the Greeks. And if the wisest and most heroic of our ancestry engaged in an unnatural vice, well that could be forgiven. To a modern warrior and to a gentleman, they would be casually forgiven.

By real men, men like John, they would simply be overlooked, if not forgiven.

He was white, sand white, with blue-green eyes and pink lips and these streaks of brown like motor oil spread through his blond hair.

And he said he was an Indian. His father was half Indian and had worked in the Bureau of Indian Affairs, and Greg owned these Navajo memories of dark men in tribal costume initiating his father into the tribe, men who came out of the desert on the reservation, came to their door in the night. He had watched them from a window in his Spider Man pajamas. So Greg kept insisting that he was an Indian.

He used phrases like "my Indian brothers and sisters," and they sounded strange from those lips and that skin and that hair.

I met him in an office at the newspaper. He was leaning against one of the broken walls, white peeling plaster, leaning and balancing back in an ancient chair and smoking a Camel.

"Pleased to meet you," he said, and you could tell automatically that this was one of those lost boys who watch their words too carefully. Guarded.

"I'd like you to help him," Pam, our editor, said when he had left.

"Help him how?"

"Train him. He's new to being an editor."

"Can he write?"

"He can write. And maybe you could talk to him."

"About?"

"Well, you're bisexual or whatever, right?"

"In theory."

"Maybe you could talk to him. I think he might be gay."

That night I talked to him. I brought him home to my new apartment and sat him down and poured him glasses of inexpensive wine and talked to him.

And the white Indian looked more like a Confederate soldier. Like some black-and-white photograph of a boy in a uniform, with red painted in at the cheeks. Natural, naturally handsome without trying, nothing extravagant.

And he loved poetry. And fictions. And sneaking to Shakespearean plays. And for all that, he was deeply ashamed. So we whispered across my rickety table about Dante, made sick jokes about Sylvia Plath; and by morning we had met Hemingway.

He never went home after that. After Hemingway.

"You look a little wrung out," John said. "Rough night?"

"Yeah, got in late," I lied, for no reason.

"Where'd you go?"

"Oh, just some . . . place. Just this place, you wouldn't know it."

"Maybe I do. What's it called?"

"I don't know. Why'd you ask? Just this place, you know? What can I say? I went to . . . a place."

"I should warn you that you're exhibiting the signs of Tourette's syndrome. Where the hell'd you go?"

"The Allegro," I lied again, because it was the only gay bar I knew about.

"The Allegro," he said, and stroked his chin as if he were an old man. "I haven't been there in years."

John made a drink with vodka and sugar and lemon and ice. He said it came from Portugal.

"My husband's in Portugal," he said. "We met here, though; in law school."

In his apartment, he wasted no space. Basic metal furniture, and shelves and books and books and books; solid-white walls and Spartan structure.

Solid white, Aegean white, the color of those days.

I pulled a tall chair up to his table, while he leaned against the counter by the blender.

"I remember what it was like for me," he said, "coming out of the closet."

"I'm already out."

"Yeah, right. Ten bucks says you've got a long history of bull-shitting yourself."

The drink was bitter, like lemon peel. He kept taking it away, making it sweeter.

"You're not ready for this."

"Who's that?" I asked, pointed to a black-and-white picture on his shelf.

"Me and my dad."

"Looks like you're happy," I said, "in the picture."

"We were. Why do you say it like that?"

"So he doesn't know about you?"

"Yeah, he knows I'm gay. Can you say that word? 'Gay'?"

"Yes I can, Mr. Rogers."

"Sorry. I've got this overwhelming urge to treat you like my little brother."

"You've got brothers?"

"Sure," he said. "A lot of 'em." Then he whispered, "They know too."

I walked around his apartment the way you pace when you don't know what to say.

"Are you sure?" I asked him. "Are you sure you're gay?"

"Why, aren't you?"

"Yeah, I'm . . . I'm resigned."

"I don't trust people who use words like 'resigned' in casual con-versation. Relax."

"Sorry."

"That's better." And he licked the stirrer with a smacking sound, took the drinks toward his bedroom.

"So when did you make the decision?" he asked when we were sitting on his bed and the television was on in the background.

"What decision?"

"*The* decision. When was the big day when you woke up and said, Well, I really like women, but—ah, what the hell? I think I'll be gay."

"You're joking."

"I'm joking."

"I've met some other guys. They were gay."

"And?"

"They were more like what you'd expect."

"And I'm not what you expected."

"You act like a guy."

"Thanks." And he lay back, resting his drink on his chest. "Let me guess: poor Scott is gay, and it's all his dad's fault."

"You're the psychiatrist."

"No. But I'm good. I'm real good." And he took on a thick German accent. "Tell to me your story."

When I finished, and had talked too much and too long and faded two or three times into this horrified whisper, so that he squinted his eyes and said, "I can't hear you," he said, "Do you know how many NFL linebackers were raised by their mothers?"

"No. You do?"

"I've met a few. But a lot of them are straight. Half the men in our generation had no father. If a disappearing dad was all it took to make you gay, we'd have one hell of a population problem."

"What is it, then?"

"You're a bright cub. You read the *Phaedrus*. Figure it out. For four thousand years men from Greece to Rome to America to Iran have realized they were gay. Men from every background, every class, every kind of family. Every psychological makeup. When they write about it or talk about it, you hear the same things over and over."

"Your point?"

"Well, it couldn't be genetics or anything. It's obviously a four-thousand-year-old conspiracy. Millions of straight men pretending to be gay to piss the normal people off."

"Are you like this with your clients?"

"I don't have any. The only observation I've been able to make is that gay men who make the same kind of peace with their fathers that every *other* guy has to make are usually pretty comfortable with being men. The others you can look for at Queer Nation rallies on CNN."

John could splash turpentine on the prettiest of fictions. A one-man wrecking crew for castles in the sky. He could make you feel like a small-minded idiot. And when you left you always thanked him for it.

"I thought you asked me up here to have sex," I said, when it was long past time to leave.

"Thought, or hoped? It doesn't matter, I'm a married man."

"And real men take their vows seriously."

"You've been listening."

And it would be stupid to try to tell anyone what is was like when he kissed me.

I went home to Greg that night because I needed absolution, because I wanted to be with him in heterosexual surroundings, my surroundings, wanted to be with him in our apartment and with whiskey and to hear him talk about women and smile my brittle smiles and know that everything was going to be alright.

I went with him because the talk was assured and preordained and our jokes slanted and self-confident, and the whiskey hid the taste of another man's mouth on my tongue.

And I drank with him because he wanted me to drink with him, and I always did whatever he wanted me to do.

We took off our shirts in the living room and sat down with the bottle between us, and I lied to him about what had happened with John Ryder.

"I took him," I said and leaned backward against the wall.

"No shit." He was fascinated and hungry.

"He wanted it," I lied again. "Guys like that—*really* gay guys— you know they want it."

"Took him like a woman?"

"As close as you can come."

Lies, lies, lies.

But if he thought that I could be like that, if he thought that I could be on top and stick it into other people like a thorn shoved out of my thighs, then maybe he could see me as just a variant, a variegated form of a man. Instead of taking it like a fucking woman.

Magic words, that's what works with Greg.

When you let yourself go, when you tighten your chest so that your voice runs low, and then you talk about Joyce or Hemingway, that is what works with Greg.

Then he's this boy, then he's sitting on the carpet by your feet while you hold a book in your hand and explain a paragraph, and you make your interpretation tough and you make it mannish and you make it mean so that he cannot feel ashamed for loving the feel of a book or for loving you or for loving poetry.

"I wish I were gay," he says one night.

"What do you mean?"

"I wish I were gay or bisexual or something."

And you don't say anything about it, you just hug him tightly, except that you do tell him that his skin is perfect, it is like stone, he is statuesque, he is Greek. But he stiffens at that, so you laugh low in your throat and pretend to shove him away, and you smile and call him friend.

And those are the words that work with Greg.

Nothing works with Greg.

You have lived with him for a year because you have loved him. You are used to him, used to all the givens, the sentence structures, the morning coffee, the midnight rum. The writing and the books and his catlike snoring in your room. He is never far away.

It is only his silence that keeps you at bay. The sudden, ice-water silence that keeps your hands in your pockets, your lips from his neck and his ears. You just kiss him in his sleep and pretend that he is awake. But you never tell him you love him, because that would mean you were really gay.

John's voice is clipped on the phone.

"You're not even kidding yourself," he says. "Why try to kid me?"

"I'm just telling you what's going on in my life."

"What's going on in your life is that you're falling in love with a straight guy. Brilliant move. Keep it up and you can graduate to cruising parks and public restrooms."

"I hate you."

"Nah. You don't."

You and Greg call your fathers on the same night, usually Friday night. You exaggerate equally, you make every small anything sound important and grand until they say, "Well done." Then you drink, your duty done.

You feel alone. You isolate yourselves in your town house in this shitty neighborhood. You feign refinement and live on beer and potatoes. You read Sam Shepard for some laughs, and you put five-dollar van Gogh prints on the walls.

On Saturday you brought home the acid.

You bought it at school from a friend.

"You've taken it before?" he asks.

"Many times." *You liar*. And he will not take it, which is good because you do not want him to. He will stand to one side, he will guide you with imagination. Reasonable and safe and sober. And you think that it could kill you, although it will not touch him.

You feel nothing for fifteen minutes, and for fifteen minutes see nothing except him, curious, with expectant eyes. Then there is a quivering in your stomach, and you hardly notice you are talking too fast, talking over him, and colors slowly shift.

"Can you see it?" he asks, guiding. "Can you see the water?"

"No. Where."

And he points to a spot on the tiles, where you can see a pool of water if you try. If you want to. And figures like fish darting underneath the surface.

You walk to it and look down into yourself. And you are a fat man, fat and bald and white and stuffed. And feminine and weak.

"It's beautiful, isn't it?" he asks from his chair.

"No," you say, but you are up, you are walking around through your rooms, looking at curtains and wood grains and laughing at your shadow.

"You can see everything!" he calls to you. "You can see the world!"

"I think something's wrong," you call back. "Maybe it's too much, too strong."

"Relax," he says. "Be yourself."

Ah, yourself. But your self is wrong when you look in the mirror. You hide behind the bathroom door and run hot water. The steam is thick and dull like lead, and there are hollow centers in your eyes.

"I think I'm dying," you say, but it is only a weak statement, expected from a faggot like yourself. Then you notice the blackness on your tongue and the plaster-of-paris teeth with metallic green devils splattered on them like bugs across a windshield. And dying can be a good, good thing.

He doesn't hear you when you scream, if you screamed. You go back into the kitchen, where he is still talking, guiding.

"They're so fucking beautiful," he says. "They're so white and pink and clean."

"Who?"

"The girls." He smiles. "All the beautiful women."

"I'm going out to the bars," I told John. "I'm going to Eager Street."

"Mistake."

"Aren't you the guy who's always telling me I have to make some mistakes?"

"There are limits."

"It'll be a learning experience."

"It'll be pain. Think you'll walk through the doors and meet the man of your dreams? He'll take you away to his castle and you'll live happily ever after like two princes in a butch fairy tale."

"Funny. Hysterical."

"Hysterical is what you'll be after they're done with you. Gay men are no different than straight men. They want what's fresh, what's new, what's never been had before. They'll eat you for lunch. Ask any woman."

"I'll take my chances."

I could have made any man into a warrior that night. There was enough beer and enough low lighting to make anyone look good.

But he didn't need the beer or the lights, didn't need my imagination. Six two or three, with ebony hair and devil black eyes, torso thick as a Roman column. He walked wide angled, connected to the ground, connected and heavy, and you thought that maybe he believed that the floor should shake a little under his boots.

I was shaking.

But I took it like a man, with my jaw hard and my back straight, cigarette pinched between thumb and forefinger, pointing out, slow-moving eyes that make no contact.

"Got a light?" I asked him, and it could have been Paramount perfect, except that on that final word, that final syllable, nerves caught up in my throat and tangled, and my voice shattered like glass.

"Your cigarette is already lit," he said, but he smiled.

"I'm not really used to this."

"No? *I* am." Easy words, breathed through smoke and a Belgian accent that I mistook for something Southern. Cajun. Familiar.

Adam's apartment was a labyrinth, dark and deep, rooms that led into other rooms, miniature staircases that moved you farther and farther underground. The subconscious, hidden beneath a row house in Fells Point. He had chosen it, he said, because of that effect and decorated it with old books and candles until it looked like a catacomb.

He was embarrassed to be a sculptor. He sneered and growled when he said it but grinned when he showed me the statues he kept in a small storeroom or lined up in his studio with its high arching walls.

"This is one of my favorites," he said and pulled off a canvas. A young man sitting, naked, while behind him a pack of wolves crept out of swirling impressionistic asphalt thunderclouds.

"I keep saying I'm going to sell it, but I can't," he said. "It belongs here."

I hate people who are obvious with their symbolism, I thought. But it was only a John Ryder thought, lost in me.

In his bedroom he lit two half-melted votive candles and put them in saucers on the floor.

"You afraid?" he asked, and then I noticed the heat. Not Floridian heat, with a cool breeze that wets you down.

"No," I said and sat down on a corner of the bed. "No. Who's afraid of the big bad wolf?"

Ball's in your court, Voltaire. Can we just do it?

Baltimore heat, urban heat, stagnant. Cooks you from the inside out. He stripped off his shirt in the heat.

"Just relax," he said, a trailing whisper. "Trust me."

He took my shirt near the waist and lifted it above my arms, over my head, undressing a child. My arms and legs shook instinctively when he slid down to his knees, put his chest against mine, soothed me backward onto his bed.

"Let it happen," he said again and again, short breaths. "Just let go."

Hot and blistering red, pressure on my lips, with an aftertaste like sharp spice, cinnamon.

And resistance was this fragile thing, this afterthought, something that melts like ice cream. His weight on my chest was heavy, hard to breathe but, by some miracle, not crushing. Thick hands kneading the muscles in my chest, smoothing down to my thighs; and my own smaller hands slid across that broad back, traced the grooves in the muscles, descended, shaking, to the curve of his lower back and circled there.

His mouth was open, full of steam, leaving wet imprints on my chin, then my chest, threatening and exciting around my belly. He reached up and ran a hand over my face, the smell of salt, and someone else kissed and licked his palm until it was clean.

And I saw it all as if from outside myself, some silent observer, drugged, drunk, running over with excruciating life.

So this, I thought, so this is what it feels like.

So this is what other men feel when they lie beside a woman for the first time. When they taste her breath and her skin, when their thoughts sprint and trip over themselves, when their hands and their bodies move in desperate rhythm, primitively, and the flesh of another human being is so soft and so flawless that it is embarrassing, your hands are profane, the spirit is willing and the flesh makes you want to weep.

"Whatever," I said. "Anything."

"That's enough," he said, and slid out of the bed. "I'll walk you to your car."

e l e v e n

Coming out.

It's like the opening of eyes. Stepping out of a room that is too dark into too much of a morning. It's the invasion of light through your eyes, stretching the pupils and thudding against your head.

Now when I walk through the campus or sit in classes, faces come into focus that I recognize. They sit beside their girlfriends or fraternity brothers, they laugh too loudly and clear their throats deeply and wear their caps backwards—rougher on Monday mornings than they looked on Friday nights. On Eager Street.

And a word takes shape, one of Honey's words, whispered, goes hissing by: "conspiracy."

And America hurts, now that I am on the other side. It is frightening, this side of the judgment seat.

Outside a gay bar, a boy disappeared. His friends rattled their keys and paced in the parking lot. There *was* no family to file a missing person's report. When they found him, someone had slashed his throat and cut up his genitals like Christmas ribbons.

Nothing was said about that on television. "A man killed near Eager Street." *No apparent motive.* They neutered him again.

Next story.

It might have been different had he been a Christian. No—it might have been different had he loved only women, had he been *only* a Christian. Or it might have been different if one of *us* had done that to one of *them*, if one of *us* had cut a boy for being only a

Christian. Then someone would have missed him. Then his mother would have looked for him, frantic in the street, and moaned over him in the alley where she found him. Then he would have been an argument for peace, an archangel, a sixteen-year-old parable, the subject of sermons and books and maybe a statue.

But it could not be like that, because he was more than a Christian.

And *we* do not cut *them*, anyway.

She is older than she pretends to be, this girl.

She leans against Greg contemptuously, I think. Leans against him and pretends not to be bothered by my smoking. I light my third.

"That's my couch," I want to say to her. "That's my couch you're lounging on."

Greg is nervous and talks between us and pours too many drinks.

"Him too," I would say, before showing her the door. "He also belongs to me."

There are veins in her legs that look like blue vines in milk. She is lost somewhere in her thirties. Early thirties. Maybe.

"I was telling Anne here about your writing," he says to me, then looks to her. "He's very good."

"Oh really? I'd love to read it."

Oh really? I'd love to kill and eat you.

"Sure." I smile. "That'd be fine."

"I write a little myself, you know," she says to him and pats his knee.

A very little, I'll bet. Let me guess: poems to your cats? I'm an old fan of epic cat poetry.

"I'd love to read them," I say.

"Oh, they're very private," she says. "I've only shown them to Greg."

Greg says nothing. I'll give him that much. He says nothing.

You can tell that she doesn't want to leave. Maybe their silence and throat clearing means that *you* should leave. But this house is mine, with everything in it. I will guard what is mine, and this house belongs to me.

"I'll walk you to your car," he says, and she says, "Fine."

He is gone a very long time.

• • •

"I want you gone," I tell him.

"What are you saying?"

"I want you to leave."

"Did I do something?"

"I'll give you a couple of days. Then you need to leave."

"Why are you doing this? Why are you doing this to me?"

"Whatever is still here that belongs to you after forty-eight hours you can look for at the Salvation Army."

"You're in love with me. You son of a bitch. You're in love with me."

"I'm in love with you. And you need to leave."

"They're sending me to Somalia," my father said. "Soon. Almost immediately."

"What about Joanne?"

"She'll be in California."

"That sucks."

"If the corps wanted us to have families, they'd have issued them."

"Right."

The talk is tight, the phone connection lousy.

"When do you leave?"

"Soon. It'll be quite the battlefield."

Like *Heartbreak Ridge*, you almost say. But that is forgotten, and my father is over that, past that, angry about leaving. And happier than he's ever been in his entire life. A battle. After Vietnam, after Lebanon, after Desert Storm. All spent waiting, watching. *Say, boys, mind if I play?* At last a battle. Sing praise to the god Mars. I say little, out of respect. Silence congratulates him for finally being baptized a marine.

I want my own baptism.

I talk to Adam, he calls and asks me to come to him. He waits while I scan his library, ask him questions. He likes that and gives me books to read. I will always and invariably love anyone who gives me books to read.

"Christ," he says, "I hate these." He sits on his bed, shirtless, holds out his arms. They are covered with drawings, elaborate and evil.

"How long have you had them?" I ask.

"Since I was seventeen. Maybe eighteen."

"They don't fit you."

"No," he said. "No, they don't. I just thought . . ."

He stood up and wrapped around me.

"I thought they would make me straight."

"Like the marines."

"Yeah, just like the marines."

He takes us to the brink again and again. Right up to the edge, and then he stops.

You stop coming, you stop calling. Then he is on the phone, then he jokes or begs. Then you are back in his bed. But your kisses become distracted, you have something to say.

"Where are you?" he asks, looking down at you.

Maybe. Maybe someday I will tell you.

After the lines and curvature of your face are more familiar, less threatening. After echoes of your gravel-pit voice stop burning through my hours and days like acid etching glass.

Then quietly, without display, I will paint for the artist a portrait of words, creating worlds. Innocence, subsiding. A child's temple filled with the smoke of your incense rising.

When we had sex his body turned to stone and unleashed its anger, burning, hurting, tearing. His gentleness sparked and flared and vanished in a burst of frenetic energy, his body pounding, and I pushed against him, sucking in air and trying to breathe.

After he was done, he slapped the back of my thigh and said, "It's getting late. You should get home."

I stood and slid my jeans on, biting rage, swallowing it. Swallowing. The room was gray, he lay naked and spread-eagled, self-satisfied, staring at the ceiling. The room was silent, where I had expected choirs of angels to sing.

"You want me to make you a sandwich or something? For the road?"

"No, thanks."

"Something wrong?"

"Nothing. It doesn't feel right. You know, I don't know. It's not what I expected."

"Never is. Sorry, you hate clichés, right?"

"Is this . . . is this the way you usually do things?"

"You got a problem?"

"I've got a problem with you."

"Why? What'd I do?"

"It was all about sex, right? You wanted to fuck me."

"Isn't that what you wanted?"

"Just wanted to get laid. What a fucking joke. Our relation-ship . . ."

"Relationship?" He sat up at that. "Jesus Christ, kid."

"I've got to go."

"I think you're forgetting something."

"This should be good. More of your wisdom. What am I forgetting?"

"You're forgetting you're just a fag."

I can fit in.

And if the way to survive is to hollow out your chest and narrow your eyes and sharpen your claws, then I can join the young lions on Eager Street.

It's warm in the press of boys and the cigarette smoke and the dance-floor laser beams.

Here anyone can become a carnivore. Here anyone can devour anyone like meat. You know the way because it is written in your bloodstream.

Never hesitate to kiss them if they are pretty. Take them out back and lean them against brick and let them run their hands across your chest and wet your lips. Then leave. When you see dawn in their eyes, cutting through the vodka fog with knifish expectations, then turn your back and walk away.

You learned it from a master.

It is still early and the old ones buy you beers. It is still early enough for free beer. And you are cold inside.

• • •

"There's nothing here for me," I say to Joanne, because I am selfish.

"It sounds like you could use a break." She should sound tired, my father gone. And in California, where she is stationed, it is late. But she talks to me, thirsty for connection, and says I could use a break.

"Florida," I say. "I can go and live with Sandy for a while. Half a year."

"OK."

"Then come back for my last semester."

"Well, it sounds like a plan."

"I could use a break."

I stand in a corner of the bar and practice indifference. Look around the room at these seamless Florida boys and the clothes and the crew cuts and all that is sanctioned by *GQ* magazine. Better clothes and superior style. But still Baltimore. Just like Baltimore. Only prettier.

An hour before, I left Sandy's house and left her cooing and smoothing out my clothes and winking at Karen, because I am young and going out for some harmless fun as she and Karen did in the fifties and sixties—that's what she thinks.

"Oh, I wish I were that young again," she says to Karen, who says something about "all that energy!"

Energy.

Because she knows I am gay and she is proud, proud, proud of me. And she has opened up her house to me in a mother's way, and in a mother's way she sees exactly what she wants to see.

Meanwhile, out there, in the middle of the music, lost in a cloud of expensive cologne, the bruised and battered boys of the thirteenth generation are dancing and playacting for one another. They look the same and dance the same and dress the same. They have rhythm. Their straight brothers, who are also just the same, are dancing with their women down the street.

Their straight brothers, unmarked, unbruised at birth, with some different chromosome, some different DNA. Difference so small you need a microscope to see through the dissimilarity. A small thread of blood that is as old at least as literature, as old at least as history, the scarlet thread of redemption that makes some boys artists and artisans and poets and musicians and philosophers and builders and warriors and coincidentally makes them love other men.

Their ancestors found one another, as these boys do; they hid or walked together openly or merged into crowds like chameleons, depending on the times and the mood swings of the clergy. They found mercy in secret congregations. And came out of their circle of brothers to splash cathedral walls with color and fill books to leather brims and shudder out the thick black notes of symphonies and create everything that everyone thereafter would point to and say, "Ah! Art! Ah! Culture! Ah! The best of Western civilization!"

Little time, for my generation. We are still Hollywood, still art, still Broadway, still Navy. But tired. Worn down and beaten, with purple speckles that start low on your body and crawl upwards like blue ladybugs stuck on your skin.

Beaten and hunted, banned from the churches and synagogues and mosques, cast out of families like old bundles of a dead uncle's clothes that went sour with mothballs in the attic *and we never liked him anyway*. Little time in us for art, no time for our best. Little room. Anger has room. Anger, and hatred in full burning bleeding springtime bloom.

And Christ, I hated the white man.

My stomach is thumping with the beat from the Dolby speakers, and tonight I am an Indian. As petrified as an Indian, as much in my tribe. Petrified of the laws that define me as felon and deviant. Petrified of the glass smiles from the round-eyes. Petrified of the midnight knock at the door. Petrified and white, frozen expression, wooden-nickel Indian.

A slim boy drew close. Bright eyes.
  "Buy you a drink?"
  "Sure," I said. "Thanks."

Should I say that we talked? That we talked about the tribe?
That would all be lies.
When I said it was time to go, he followed me.

His apartment was neat, almost clinical. A television was on, I sus-
pected it played eternally, with the sound shut off. Company, probably. A handsome boy, but he needed company.

We undressed in silence beside the bed. His skin was clear and
fresh, I thought it looked comforting. The air-conditioning was running high, high enough to blast frost up the windows, so his heat
relaxed more than excited me.

You never practice safe sex. Not since Adam. Not anymore. No
need for a condom because you never enter another body and no
one enters you. Paranoid sex, because you hardly take off your
clothes. Every man for himself. You had paranoid sex with him in
a shadow of a connection. I had paranoid sex and we fell asleep.

So what was so different in the morning?

Just that he looked like an angel swaddled up next to me. Lips
parted slightly, eyes fluttering. I stroked his hair and kissed his cheek
until he stirred, and held him tightly while he breathed.

"I didn't think you'd still be here," he said.

"I'm here," I said. "I am."

Then we made love again, because of his lips and his eyes and
the way that he breathed. We made love, as I had with the first pain
and the first lover.

But we were safe.

We made love in a bed in a state where we could have gone to
jail for making love, could have lost our jobs, could have had our
rights politely "suspended"—a temporary measure, for public safety,
for public morality—human rights "suspended" in America; we
made love under that kind of storm cloud. But we had condoms on
our dicks, so we were safe.

And then dressed separately as if to be modest, two strangers who
had spent a night together with no more than a handful of words,
an introduction. For modesty's sake we dressed separately.

• • •

He went into the bathroom, while I looked for my socks. I accidently overturned a duffel bag on an armchair. And then a bottle fell out and cracked and rattled while he stepped quickly back into the room, the trapped little rabbit.

"What are these?" I ask.

No answer from the rabbit.

"If this is AZT," I whisper, as if he has just become holy, "I think I'm going to kill you."

"You've seen it before?" he asks, nonchalant.

Hell.

And the hatred burned up like seltzer in my throat.

Hell is next, boy. Hell is closer than you think.

And I wanted to stand up and walk over to him and pound my fist into him again and again and again, pound my fear out into him, draw it out of myself and put it into him and make him suffer, make him hurt and bleed.

My sister Lisa and I had taken cardboard boxes from her closet and arranged them around her room. Her room, with its pretty pink shades and girlish white furniture, with white lace around the borders of her bed.

She set out a tea set, a few stolen dishes from the kitchen, on top of one of the boxes, and she argued with me about the rules to the game.

"You're the husband," she mandated. "And I've just finished cooking dinner, and then . . . and then you come walking in home from work. OK?"

"I don't want to do this," I whined.

"OK, you're just coming home now from work, OK? OK, so now . . . you go outside and then come walking in."

I stepped reluctantly outside her bedroom door, then walked back inside.

"I'm home!" I bellowed.

"OK, dinner's ready," she said, infinitely pleased that I was playing.

I knelt beside the cardboard box, and she pretended to bring a tray of food over from a fictitious kitchen.

"OK, now you can eat."

She stood nearby, hands folded, as I gulped forkfuls of air.

"Well? How do you like it?"

"This food is cold!" I said.

"It is not!"

"I said it's cold, woman!"

"Quit it! You're not playing right."

I stood up and approached her, menacingly.

"If I say it's cold, it's cold!"

And I slapped the air around her face, and she caught on and thrust her head from side to side as if she could feel the blows. And then we both laughed, because we were acting like adults.

We were just playing house. Playing home.

Children do as they have been shown. And one of the bruised boys had beaten me. Tossed my life like dice, because that was what he had been shown.

Because he was just like me.

And I walked to him as he leaned against the wall, and pulled him close and cried tears, unashamed. I still do not understand.

I understood the rest, because it is what you get. When you give in to the sin, you deserve what you get.

"I'm dying," I said to Sandy. "I'm dead."

Is it some kind of hobby of yours, you little shit, splattering terror on her face?

"What do you mean?" she asked, and I noticed that when she is hit, she can physically deflate.

"I'm as good as in my grave."

I slept that night in Bill's old room and imagined death. Clear the mind. Think nothing. The capital *N* kind of Nothing. Watched the window, consorted with fallen angels on his waterbed.

It's right here, in the bloodstream. Gimme an *H* and an *I* and a *V* . . .

Hell, boy. Hello.

Hi, guys. Come on in. Welcome back. I was just thinking that it could look like water in the bloodstream. Out of place and invisible in all the red. Uncomfortably out of place. So it collects somewhere, it gathers itself into a puddle or a pool, maybe in your rib cage, maybe behind your ear, maybe in an arm or a leg. It gathers there and gathers strength and gathers itself up on its haunches and waits.

We marked you. We own you. We're here to collect.

You won't have long to wait.

"It wasn't supposed to be you," Bill said. "It should've been me."

We drank Big Gulps like teenagers and drove around our old streets.

"How's that?"

"I should've been the—I should've been gay. No father. Raised by lesbians, for Christ's sake. Rodney was an asshole, but at least he should have made you straight."

Bill took the car to the parking lot next to the Bible college, parked it under a street lamp.

"It's getting late," he said. He coughed and took another drag from his cigarette.

"We're getting old," I said. "You look older, at least."

"Fuck you."

After Bill lost Jesus, he picked up a bottle, because that's what the preachers always said would happen to you. If you ever left, if you ever became unsaved, you would become involved in something. Bill became involved with his bottle and Bill had loved his bottle and Bill had used his bottle to fill up the God-shaped hole in his chest. Until it turned on him, until it almost killed him, until it put him to sleep on the floor of his apartment and he almost didn't wake up.

Months of therapy under lock and key before he stopped listening to the mental recordings of preachers, before he said he could live minute to minute without the Church of God or a drink. He talked then about living day to day as if it were surreal, a far away goal and a dream. But he won; even if now he did look older in *that* way: day to day.

"I don't know about you," he said. "I don't know how you look."

"No?"

"Nah. I guess you look a lot like your mother."

When you're standing and talking to a grave, exactly one half of you believes that someone is listening. You are five or six or seven, clinging to some adult's storybook answer to one of your questions, and full color has kicked in to your imagination, so you even *see* the pretty prayers popping like bubbles up into heaven. The other half feels dense because you are standing there talking to dirt.

I look like you. In the eyes, they say. Never noticed that until you were dead.

You're dead. I forget that all the time. It's more real now because I think I may be joining you.

A faulty condom brought me into this world; think that's what'll take me out? Ah, but you don't think that's funny.

I don't know. I act like you. That's not bad, it just hurts.

If you can hear me, if you can do anything, if you can pull any strings. Let me do something. Let me learn something before I go.

There was nothing like a flower anywhere on or near her grave. No white stone marker, no detailed board, no stylized writing. A flat bronze plaque.

MICHELLE, it read. And that was the end.

Strange for a woman who loved so many men. Who looked under every handsome face, rough back, and angry set of hands for someone who could change her name, make a connection.

Sandy pounded on the door to Bill's room too early in the morning to really be believed.

"Up!" her happy morning-person voice chirped. "Up, up, up!"

"Go to hell," I returned in the same voice, all daffodils and sunshine.

"You've got a phone call," she said. "It's Joanne."

He's dead.

"I talked to your father," she said. "He said he'll pay for your last semester. If you can tear yourself away from Florida."

"I'll pack. Thanks."

"Thank your father. It's his money."

"Right. You had nothing to do with this."

"Not this time. Not really. Give him some credit."

"You're right. Sorry." That was just a slip, an echo. All accounts are paid.

I have a small room on campus at the University of Maryland.

There is no space, it is a shoe box with a tiny window. So everything here is in its own place, there are no accidents, every item is chosen. I spend a great deal of time, between classes and food that is prepackaged, straightening the pens in my drawer, sorting my socks by color and then by size and finally by textile. It is big enough for order, and it is a small enough space for perfection.

"One last time then," my new friend says. "One last time to Eager Street."

I have new friends, good friends. Young and serious and gay. "Coincidentally gay," some of them say, seriously.

"Come on, man," he says. "I don't want to go alone. It's Saturday night. I just want a drink. I'm not looking for anyone."

The same faces stream by, lift their eyebrows, try hard to look tough. Newer boys, stronger. Some of them happy. Either they were not here before or I could not see them.

"What am I doing here?" I ask my friend, because it is the sort of thing he expects me to say. But I am unconvinced.

"Relax," he says. "Maybe your soul mate is waiting for you over by the pool tables."

"My soul mate doesn't shoot pool. At least not in a place like this. You'll never meet the right guy in a place like this."

And then a new voice says, "Hi. I'm the right guy."

Bobby. His name is Bobby Hampson, but when I talk about him to my friends, he's Bobby Handsome or Bobby with the baseball cap. And I don't care when they roll their eyes.

"So where do you want to go?" he asks on our first date.

"I don't know." And I almost say, "I'm not sure what I want," or, "I don't know where this is going," or something metaphorical and wasteful and profound, but that would have fallen on the asphalt and bounced away.

His apartment is small. One bedroom, a living room, mostly empty. He has stacks of records and books and CDs, and the walls are covered with neat rows of old baseball photographs. He speaks reverently of baseball, as if it is ancient and Byzantine, as if it is his religion. He is all motion, this Bobby, he talks through excitement and plays his favorite songs like a DJ, explains their significance to his life as if I would be interested. And I am interested.

"I'm talking too much," he says. "I know I'm talking too much. You're never going to come here again. But since you're here, now, listen to this . . ."

"I don't want to have sex," I say, out of breath and out of context after we have kissed on the floor for a long time.

"Ever again?"

"No. Never."

"Reason?"

"It's a waste of energy."

"That's alright," he says when he stands up. "We'll wait until we're in love."

So he had the gift of prophecy. And who am I to argue with a prophet?

The wide-screen TV in the campus Pub flickered and warped colors, and you could hardly make out the fat man with the beard, who explained patiently and piously why little boys should be able to have sex with big fat grown men. He talked about his rights and about some organization, the North American Man/Boy Love Association, NAMBLA for a catchy acronym, and then the camera switched to scenes of a police raid of some pedophile's house, with close-ups on the cardboard boxes full of teddy bears and Vaseline.

And when it was done and the dried-up voice of a news team

meteorologist announced rain for the rest of the evening, the editorial staff of the *Retriever* turned as if in slow motion and looked solidly at me.

Because I am their gay friend, I am the gay person, I am the Gay. And all "gays" must know one another the way all "blacks" know one another, and we've probably all slept with one another, and I am expected to make some defense for what they have seen and what they wish they had not seen, because in their world I am the Gay.

"That man," I growl, and point my cigarette at the screen, "is the best argument I can make for lethal injections."

And they laugh after a pause. Laughter nervous and guilty, the way you laugh when you hear a joke about Jews from a rabbi.

"And I thought I was a homophobe," Pat, the editorial manager, said.

"I'm not a homophobe. I love gay men."

More laughter.

"You know what I mean. I just don't understand why we let these self-appointed spokespeople make us look like we're everything Anita Bryant ever said we were."

"I didn't think you were allowed to say things like that," he said.

"What do you think we are? A social club? A political party? Scientology? Do you think I'll have to turn in my membership card?"

And I'm relieved by their laughter. I draw in their attention and their laughter. I feel like a preacher.

"I think a hell of a lot of heterosexuals are into cross-dressing or getting their asses whipped or whatever. They just don't do it in the middle of Main Street USA in front of a CNN camera and pretend it's a political statement. If they're into that shit, then fine—but what the hell's it got to do with being gay?"

And heads nod, and the conversation opens, and there is that sensation of release when you talk about whatever it is that you did not think you were allowed to talk about. And I'm not offended by questions, and I censor nothing, and I can't believe the ways some of my friends have quietly misunderstood me and made false assumptions—"You're a fucking *Republican?*"—and never would have known, because professional homosexuals had already told them what to think about me, about gays, about men like me, and because they didn't know they could ask questions or tell me what they believe or tell me why they believe it.

"As a therapeutic gesture," Pat says after I have talked too hard and too long. "Therapeutic for us, I mean—why don't you write about this? In the *Retriever*."

"Nah, I'm not an editorialist."

"I'll make an exception. Just keep it polite."

"Your article was horrendous!"

James LaBelle, the official campus activist, the politically correct crusader, the white-bread boy wonder of any and all postmodern causes, charged at me in my dorm room.

"Which article?"

"Your little exercise in internalized homophobia."

"Ah, let's see . . ." And I don't like him, so I can say what I want with nothing to lose. "An internalized homophobe—that's any guy who disagrees with a Queer National, right? Or any guy who disagrees with . . . well, with you."

"Oh, I see where you're coming from," he said. "You're a disgrace to anyone who's ever put themselves on the front lines for the cause."

"No," I say, and I am bouncing in my tennis shoes, enjoying this, because I can win this argument, because he's not used to conversations and confrontation and he's not used to anything I would call free speech. He reads the right books and tries very hard to believe, he practices what to believe. And I think I may be a bully, but I am enjoying this, I am happy, happy, happy. "But I *am* a substantial threat to anyone who's ever made a jackass of themselves on the front lines. For the cause."

"If you don't like the movement," he says, "why don't you get involved?"

"I think I just did. And now that I've chirped in with the rest of you, you'd rather I'd stayed in the closet, right?"

We banter and debate, and he follows me around my apartment, and he obviously hates it when I smile.

"You just want to replace the existing social tyranny with white gay male tyrants." And now he's getting nasty.

"There's tactic number two. If you question the grand gay oompahs of the queer establishment"—and I put feminine venom in the words "queer" and "establishment"—"then you're a racist and a misogynist by default. I'll take 'Further Bullshit' for a thousand, please, Alex."

"You will regret this," he says when he is convinced that I am damned, and he is shaking his head and ready to leave. "You'll regret this. You'll see."

And that would have been nothing, a small petty nothing, if this had not been the same James LaBelle who had turned to me in the Pub the week before and said, "Wasn't that your dad on TV? The big butch marine?"

"Yeah."

"Interesting." And he smiled like a Queer National or a Baptist, what's the difference.

"I wouldn't worry about it," Kelley said.

"I don't know. I've just got this feeling."

"No one is going to care who your dad is. And James won't go to the media. Even if he did, he'd get blown off. They're not going to waste their time. There's no story here."

"You're right. I'm blowing this way out of proportion. It's not like he made a direct threat."

"No, you just hit him in the balls and he's mad as hell."

"You're right. I know you're right."

"I mean, your dad's not even involved in gay issues.

Dear Scott,

Hi, hope things are going well. Everything is fine here, except for the bombs.

By the way, didn't you do some research on gay issues for the *Retriever*? Could you send me some of your copy? I hope to testify before the Senate Armed Services Committee in May, and I could use the info. I've gotten used to making headlines and think I could have some real fun with this one.

See you soon.

Love, Dad

I want to love you.

I really want to. When we lie here again for another night and you do not touch me, that is when I want to love you.

"I want you to meet my family," you say. "They're great."

"Who do you want to say that I am?"

And you looked as if you did not understand.
"What do you mean? My boyfriend."

So I meet your handsome brother, who is in the Army. And he does not flinch when I shake his hand. And he jokes with you about the look in your eyes, and then *I* do not understand.

And I meet his wife, Lee. And she tells me about her life, before I ask, tells me about falling asleep in Vietnam, and crawling away from mortar fire.

Then in the commissary, she overhears some grizzled woman with white chicken skin whisper, "Fuckin' slopes." She knows. She understands. She is different in America.

"Do what you got to do to stay alive," she says.

"I just met you, but I feel like we're friends."

Then an exhaled stream of smoke from her sweet menthol cigarette.

"You got to be careful," she says, worried and unsmiling. "OK? You promise me?"

Puts a small strong hand on my arm.

"You're different. Different can make you dead."

She says this beautifully, lyrically, *slanted*, in a tangled English that would make good Southern Christian boys laugh.

And then there are their children, who crawl and tumble all over us, crowd around us while we play cards, confident and oblivious to their inheritance. It will be there for them when they need it.

I want to love you, and I love your family.

"It's hard for you," he says. "Is it just hard for you, or don't you want to be with me?"

"The guy who marries me won't have a husband," I say. "He'll have a mission field. That's what my pastor always said."

"So maybe I have a calling."

But I was born and bred to be a pharisee. There will always be a part of me that rears up in judgment and rages. Makes these mental charts of morality. At least I am not . . . I am better than . . . There will always be this something inside that believes the whole world is damned.

"Even you?" he asks.

"Especially me."

But I don't want to be so dark, and I don't want to say these things. I want to soothe you, love you, scoop you up in two arms like fresh branches.

"I love you," I say. Because you said it first.

And then you are with me. With me in the bed. Warm and breathing, and this is not sweat, it is not pain and hot clenched muscles and panic and fear. This is not clutching, desperation, or kettledrum heartbeats.

And I am suddenly glad to be gay.

Now is the perfect time. This is the moment.

"So, uh . . . the cats. How are those cats?"

"They're fine." Joanne and I have had a wonderful conversation. It went through all the cycles, beginning, middle, and end. And still I keep talking.

"And your nephew. What was his name?"

"Jay."

"Jay! Jay, great kid. How is he?"

"Fine. Just fine."

"Well, it was great talking to you."

"You too. Bye."

And then there is silence and much smoking and pacing. I dial her number again.

"I, uh . . . are you sure you're OK?"

"Of course, Scott. What's the matter? You don't sound good."

"No, I'm fine."

"Trouble with your roommate? What did you say his name was?"

"Bobby. Robert. Bobby. No, everything is just fine. I'm sorry I called back."

And then her phone rings again. This is not how you are supposed to do this.

"Joanne? We need to talk."

"Well, I don't know what to say," my father says. "It's not disastrous. In fact, it strengthens my position."

Joanne and I had agreed that if he really was called to testify, she would tell him. Tell him quickly. Tell him quickly and let me know what he says, when I'm safely in Brazil.

And then he was home. I knew he was home; even if she hadn't told me, I think I would have known it.

"I didn't want you to hear it this way," I said. "Not that I'm embarrassed about who I am. Not that this is that much a part of who I am . . . I don't know, I wanted to tell you face to face."

Don't testify.

"It's alright. It doesn't matter."

Please don't testify.

"I don't even know if I'm just panicking. It's just that I've ticked off a lot of activists. And I keep having this nightmare where you step out of the courtroom and get swarmed with reporters asking you if you knew your own son was gay."

"That could get ugly. I'm glad you told me. Like I said, it strengthens my position."

I won't ask you. I will not ask you.

"They'll have trouble accusing me of being a bigot when I tell them I have a homosexual son."

Please don't testify.

"I can usually smell a news story," he said. "The hounds will jump on this. You'll get your chance to speak your mind."

I will not ask you. This is something you should know.

"Sounds good," I said. But then I have always and invariably been a liar.

After Schwarzkopf, interest waned.

I sat in our living room, staring blankly at C-Span, pale faced, while the blood in my temples played a quick rhumba.

My father was tan, Somalia tan, almost an Indian.

"I don't really have a prepared statement," he began, his hands folded and working nervously. And then the camera panned away. Voices came in over him. Coverage was done for the day.

"Thank you, God," Bobby said, covering his face with his hands. I breathed for the first time in two days.

"That was a close one," I said. "That was really close."

• • •

By the time I got to the *Retriever* there was a hysterical secretary and a stack of pink memo messages waiting for me.

"What's going on?" she asked.

"Nothing," I said. "Just ignore it. Nothing."

"Really? The networks are setting up in the back room. They'd like to see you for a moment. Just tell them it's nothing."

Thirty interviews in two days.

I haven't slept or eaten in two days. And I never before knew that coffee was a hallucinogen.

"So," another nameless and faceless reporter says, "you haven't actually heard your father's testimony?"

"No," I said. "I missed it."

"Here, read this," he says, and hands me a long transcript. He keeps the camera rolling to catch the expression on my face.

I have a son.

He's an honor student at the University of Maryland. He's about to graduate. I love him as much as I love any of my sons. I respect him. But if he were to actively seek a commission in the military, I would counsel him against it, and I would fight it. There is no place in the military for him. Because my son Scott is a homosexual.

And there was more. He would be afraid for my life, that's what he said. Straight men might kill me, and it wouldn't matter if I was a good marine, if I loved my country, if I acted with honor and propriety. I was a fag, and so they would kill me. And that was clearly wrong. I was clearly wrong for the military.

And then there was something about what would happen if we were let in. Something about a bathhouse. He would want to throw his stripes over the gate onto the White House lawn because men like me, men like his son whom he so deeply respected, would turn the corps into a big bathhouse fuck fest. Because that's what fags do, after all. You might love them, you might respect them, but that's really what they do. Everyone knows that.

• • •

"Well, looks like I was a hit," he says. "How are you holding up?"

Condescending to call the bathhouse?

"Fine. Just fine. I'm talking to everyone. Anyone who will listen."

"Maybe you can get some job leads out of this."

Maybe I'll get a bullet in my back.

"I'll certainly try. How are you?"

"OK. Hiding out. Are we going to do this *CBS This Morning* satellite hookup tomorrow?"

"Sure." *So what does a bathhouse look like? I've never seen one, I've never been in one, I've never known anyone who went in one.* "Sure, if you'd like."

"Yeah, may as well."

You must know. I wouldn't know, I haven't had much sex. How many women have you had? Quick, before you hand in your stripes—how many women have you had?

"I got a call," he said. "From a producer. He's interested in a movie of the week."

You sold me. You sold my ass.

"A movie?"

Do you think they'll applaud you? For not hating your son? For not "approving," not "accepting," not "condoning"—for recognizing the sleaze and the scum and the refuse that should be kept out, Keep the Buggers Out, *out with the trash—but loving and respecting, all the same?*

"Yeah. It'd be good for a couple of bucks. Enough to get one of my kids through college. Retire. I wouldn't mind letting them do the Fred Peck story."

Loving him, even in his bathhouse.

"The Fred Peck story?"

Loving him, even him. But for Christ's sake, don't let him or his kind in. Don't let them in. Respect them on the other side of your bayonet.

"Has a ring to it. What do you think?"

Make your movie. Call it The Miracle Worker. *How I balance my love with my mistake. At last, the Fred Peck story.*

"We would like you to come and retrieve your belongings."

Honey's voice was her best Judith Martin—sterling silver and Queen Victoria and madame in a polite rage.

These were the times when she said "shan't."

"Alright," I said. "How have you been?"

"Tuesday morning at ten o'clock sharp," my grandfather's voice made its grand entry. He didn't do it as well.

"Alright, that will be fine. Would you like me to . . ."

"Please come to the backdoor," he said. "You won't step foot inside our house. I will put them outside."

"Fine. I'll see you at ten."

He met me at the backdoor and spoke through me to the friend I had brought along for help.

"Take everything in this area," he said and pointed to a corner of the basement. Then he moved to a wall and crossed his arms.

Everything was still inside the house, and my feet were touching the sacred ground. When he walked, the movement in his hips betrayed him. He had received his orders, and he had wanted to put it all outside, such a crucial part of the symbol and the orchestration. But he couldn't lift it, because he was an old and tired man.

"This place is really giving me the creeps," my friend said. "What is this, the Addams family?"

No, not really. Just an old tired man and his saint, and they don't want a faggot taking care of them.

When we went in for the final load, the floorboards creaked. Quick and furiously.

Could there be a room somewhere in some possible universe, with hardwood floors and autumn sunlight and the aqua wallpapering that she likes, where Honey and I could sit and talk and she could make her Darjeeling tea for us to drink with little German ghosts?

Tonight it's a ghost.

I unpack the boxes carefully, cut with a razor through the thick brown masking tape, and grieve. Maudlin, wasted, masturbatory—cardboard boxes and mothball grief.

Honey has given me back too much, and she has done it carelessly. Here are my books—little books with gold bindings and covers with spectacular red-and-blue trains and ducks and puppies. My name misspelled in crayon on the first page. She always let me do that.

"You have to take care of books," she said solemnly. "You have to take care of books more than anything."

And in her library she practiced what she preached. She lined the walls with books, from the stacks on the floor to the dusted shelves, mounted with screws and bolts and nails, going up to the ceiling. And she would walk down the staircase so late at night that it almost qualified as morning—in the aqua muslin nightgown that she had had since the fifth or sixth day of creation—and walk into her library. Carefully, she would flick on one light, just a small one, pretend for a second to look for something, and then just stand there in silence, breathing.

I understood and understand.

Christ, how final.

We talked more about books, and the care and maintenance of books, in the room with the light and the tea and the ghosts. In the real world, she just shoved them back into me.

I understand.

My father is my family. My family, who, at a press conference says, "Some people have children who arc born with spinal meningitis. I just happened to have a son who was born gay." And then he smiles, like a saint or a martyr, like the brave, loving father of something unlovable and defective. And I hate him for it. Or something like hate.

Because no one will ever kill my father for loving Joanne. For loving her, for holding her, for being willing to lay down his life for her. No one will hunt him down, or shoot him, or kick him out of his precious Corps, or burn his house, or beat him, or spit in his face, or mock him, or take his children away from him, or cut him, or tell him he will never see heaven, or tell him that he is a defect, or tell him that he is not an American, or a Christian, or a man.

I hate him because that is my future, for loving Bobby; those are the threats hanging over us, every second of every day, from now until the day we die. And his star-studded testimony will prolong that, will let it continue, will make it worse. Will legitimize prejudice and give hatred a handsome all-American face. This is the future he has helped guarantee for me, and the ten million boys who will come after me.

My father will never come close to understanding that, because he is safe, he is still a citizen and a good Christian and a good American. And so the world looks safe to him. I understand that the world is not safe. I understand that, and Bobby understands that. My father sees no reason to understand.

And I think there is nothing more brutal than that word, "family." And then, in the next second, I want to forgive, understand, excuse, repent, agree, anything, anything, in any direction, because there is still nothing more beautiful than the promise of that word, family.

And I loved you, Bobby, when you just walked into our room and sat on our bed, and said, "I love you. But I don't understand your family."

And then I could say, "You *are* my family."

Sit down with your anger.

Sit with it and cradle it and let it coil around you with its thick, comforting fur and nuzzle you with warm cat breath.

Sit down with your anger and begin again. Anger is an art form, like the clipping and tying of tiny Japanese trees. Cutting off the circulation, but carefully. Slowly.

Once. This once, you could have been a father to me.

Ah, remember? Remember? You have thought these words before, you have tightened these bands before. Remember.

Did you stop to think what it would do to my life? I mean, after it was over and you were gone? After you finally had the praise you have always felt born to? After the awestruck words from the masses you have always secretly despised? After you made your handfuls of headlines, took your polite bows, and were gone?

James LaBelle would call later, much later, and say he didn't mean it. Say he might have said those things or something like those things—hypothetically, I suppose, just a political statement. But he said it wasn't a threat. It wasn't the same as a threat, and he said I should have known that.

But I didn't know then.

This has nothing to do with being a human being, or having a history, or being alive. This is media, and twenty million people are watching, glancing up from their newspapers and their coffee, and they want to hear you sing.

Give them a show.

Bobby stands behind me when he can, when he is allowed. He keeps a running list of interviews and times and street corners to wait on for the next limo or taxi to arrive. We are next to each other like Siamese twins until the producer pulls me over and clips on the wires and shoves me into the light.

Then it is concentration, planning out answers to all possible questions, holding out your chin, keeping your shoulders straight and remembering everything every professor ever told you. Not the textbooks or the lectures—remember those rare honest conversations in the Pub over beers.

"We've got about a minute," a bored voice says. Who could be bored in this industry? How many twenty-million-people mornings would it take before you woke up and said, Ah, shit, here goes another day?

"Check the satellite. You there, Colonel Peck?"

"Yeah. For unknown reasons."

"Let's get a picture."

And then my father's face is on a screen to my left. Flickering, decapitated, he is pulling at the wires around his collar inside a little black box.

"You look like shit," he says.

"Thanks, Dad." We talk over the other voices in the wires.

"When'd you get those big doughlike bags under your eyes?"

"They're not real. I'm using them to hide a couple of AWOL gay marines."

We're on in five . . . four . . . three . . .

And then we're clearing our throats and sharpening our eyes and straightening our backs and trying very hard to define a good father and a good son and a good marine.

"He's really short," my dad said when Ted Koppel's voice boomed through our earpieces. "Five feet, maximum."

And everything was in perspective.

Bobby and I took a late flight to San Diego to do *Nightline*. We could have done it from Washington, but I wanted to see him. My father. I wanted to have him in the same room, I wanted to see him.

But we had come in late, and Joanne met us at the door in her bathrobe, her thick glasses. And she smiled and shook Bobby's hand. And I was reminded that my father had made one beautiful choice.

And then he came downstairs. Not the tan marine. Just the middle-aged father with white legs and reading glasses, flip-flopping in his slippers.

Mortal. Just a man.

We sat very still and answered Koppel's questions. He asked me about children. How could I be a father?

"I've had a wonderful example," I said. And this was not media, this was not PR. "Joanne and I aren't related by blood, but she has always been a mother to me. She made a home for me. I would hope I could do the same for a daughter or a son. I would know how to be a father."

And my father was nervous, talking to the small man with the big voice on the other end of the satellite beam. I don't remember what he said. He did the best he could.

The interview finished and the crew slowly packed their gear and went home.

We went out to dinner, and strangers came up to our table, interrupting us, sending us wine and waving to us from across the restaurant. They wanted to shake our hands, they wanted to congratulate us for being a family. As if that was something unusual, something rare. I guess it is. We appreciated them, but there was still no room for discussion.

At home we sat outside on the veranda. Joanne brought glasses and a bottle of red wine.

We sat for long minutes in silence, watching the ocean, the stars, soaking in the breeze and the smell of the flowers Joanne has planted by the porch.

And on one of those breezes, some gentle angel must have come. She must have walked between us, she must have seated herself in the empty chair.

Because we began to speak, and the panic and the noise of the previous weeks dissipated into thin air.

We talked about our lives, we talked about how Bobby and I met, what we meant to each other.

"So, how should I introduce you?" my father asked Bobby. "Let's see . . . how about 'son-in-law'? My son-in-law. Yeah, that fits."

The conversation was smooth, easy, natural. A natural, living thing. Our hearts and minds grew calm; I don't know if it was the Holy Spirit or the wine.

Somewhere in this night the earth is heard to whisper. The ground speaks upward through the soles of our feet and echoes the message of angels and desert prophets. The secret lingers by us, waiting to be heard. Everything is in its orbit, everyone lives in their cycle. Everything is justified, there is no angry Someone keeping score. Everything is justified and everyone is healed, eventually.

There were three men in my life, and two of them were fictions. Now there is one by my right hand, and one by my left, and another above me in the sky. And tonight they are very, very real. Tonight there is healing.

I left home looking for my father like the rest of my generation. Like the rest of every generation. We expected him to provide the panacea; we expected him to heal. Instead we found our fathers no stronger than we, no more complete. Only fragile men, the sons of other fathers in the wreckage of other dreams. When we can, we father each other.

Somewhere in this night there is a God who understands.

Somewhere our mothers still wait and pray in the language of angels.

Acknowledgments

For their support and, above all, their faith, many thanks to my editors, Bill Rosen and Mark Chimsky; Chuck Antony, the da Vinci of copy editors, who stole all my commas and will probably find fault with this paragraph; and the amazing Gillian Sowell.

And for those who hold share in these matters and these memories, all love and acknowledgment is given: my patient sleepy love, Robert Hampson; Sandy, for giving me Karen and Bill and poetry; Kelley for late-night forgiveness and coffee; Dr. Lucille McCarthy, whom I have never thanked properly; and of course Lisa, for the week on Bear Creek Road with our tender memories and your two beautiful children, unafraid.